JavaScript

For Complete Beginners

A Step by Step Self-Teaching Guide for
Learners Completely New to Programming

IKRAM HAWRAMANI

2018

STEWARDS
PUBLISHING

STEWARDS PUBLISHING

COPYRIGHT © 2018 IKRAM HAWRAMANI

FIRST EDITION

FIRST PUBLISHED IN 2018

THIS BOOK IS AN EXPANDED VERSION OF THE AUTHOR'S *COMPUTER PROGRAMMING FOR COMPLETE BEGINNERS*

HAWRAMANI.COM

About the Author

Ikram Hawramani is a veteran web designer and developer who has been building websites since 2001. He has worked as a full stack web developer and lead engineer for startups and now runs his own web publishing business. His other technical works include *Cloud Computing for Complete Beginners, HTML & CSS for Complete Beginners* and *Object-Oriented PHP Best Practices*.

This page intentionally left blank

Contents

This page intentionally left blank

1. An Introduction to Programming

Programming is the art and science of telling computers what to do. Unlike humans, computers in general have no preconceived notions of their own. You cannot command a computer-controlled robot to wash the dishes because it has no ability to understand human language, and even if it could, it has no idea what washing is, what dishes are, and how one goes about performing dish washing. By bringing together dozens of programmers, an entrepreneur can build a robot that can understand human speech and that can wash dishes. Usually each programmer works only on a small part of such a project; one team might work on writing the code that helps the robot's computer understand human speech, another might work on the code that tells the robot how to move its body parts.

Computers are incapable of learning, but they are capable of following instructions. Programming is how we write those instructions.

One question that beginners to programming often ask is "What language should I learn?" The answer is that it does not really matter. All computer programming works on the same principles, therefore if you get really good at one programming language, you can easily move from one language to another. This book uses JavaScript to teach you programming because it is a language that is used everywhere (almost every website and smartphone app uses it, for example), because using it does not require installing special software on your computer, and because it provides learners with an easy way to create drawings and other visual effects that help you really understand the way programming works.

In order to delve into JavaScript, we first need to introduce a related computer language known as HTML, which is not a programming language, but a markup language. HTML is quite simple and can be introduced in a few pages. There is no need to master HTML in order to get into programming with JavaScript, a very rudimentary understanding is sufficient.

To begin, I will show you how to create a webpage on your computer and how to put a bit of JavaScript inside it. This will show you how easy it is to get into using JavaScript regardless of what system you are using. Soon after I will introduce you to a learning environment that helps you use JavaScript without needing to deal with files. I will use a Microsoft Windows computer in this example. In the rest of the book it does not matter what system you use, the examples will work the same way on every system.

A webpage is a document (i.e. a file on a computer) that uses the HTML language to "markup" its contents. When the document is placed on a "server", people typing the server's web address (such as royalsociety.org) inside their web browsers will be able to view the document. When browsing the web, whether it is Facebook, Google or Apple.com that you are viewing, you are always viewing a webpage created with HTML.

HTML stands for Hypertext Markup Language. HTML was designed to solve the problem of telling computers how to display a document. Below is a screenshot of a typical computer file before the invention of HTML. The file was created almost 50 years ago, on April 7, 1969. It belongs to a series of documents called RFCs which have continued to this day. These documents are used by the maintainers of the Internet to discuss the development of the infrastructure and technologies related to it.

```
Network Working Group                                    Steve Crocker
Request for Comments: 1                                          UCLA
                                                          7 April 1969


                        Title:   Host Software
                        Author:   Steve Crocker
                        Installation:   UCLA
                        Date:   7 April 1969
             Network Working Group Request for Comment:   1


        CONTENTS

        INTRODUCTION

            I. A Summary of the IMP Software

                Messages

                Links

                IMP Transmission and Error Checking

                Open Questions on the IMP Software

           II. Some Requirements Upon the Host-to-Host Software

                Simple Use
```

Notice how bland the document looks. This is because it is a "plaintext" document. It is made up of alphabetical characters, numbers, spaces and a few other things. There is no room for creating borders, colors, bold and italic text, and beautiful and complex designs.

As the Internet developed and the World Wide Web was created, there was a need for the ability to create more sophisticated documents. The HTML language was created to fulfill this need. It allows us to make text bold and italic, to show images, and to create links that take users from one document to another. Later, JavaScript was created to fulfill the need for making webpages interactive and dynamic, enabling the creation of things like sophisticated web apps and games.

The way HTML works is that you write code that tells the computer how to display a document:

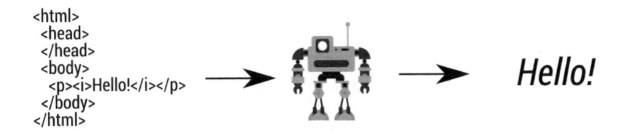

```
<html>
  <head>
  </head>
  <body>
    <p><i>Hello!</i></p>
  </body>
</html>
```

Above, on the left-hand side we have some HTML code. When this code is seen by a computer/robot, it understands it as an instruction to print the word "Hello!" in italics. On the right-hand side we have the result of what the computer will print out.

On an ordinary computer, you can type out HTML code using text-editing programs like Notepad, Wordpad, TextEdit and others, save the file as an HTML document, then open the file in a web browser (such as Google Chrome, Mozilla Firefox, Microsoft Edge or Apple Safari) to have your computer "interpret" the HTML and display the results.

There are, therefore, two "sides" to an HTML document. There is the code that defines the document (shown on the left-hand side above), then there is the "result", on the right-hand side, which is what the document actually looks like. It is the computer's job to read the code, interpret it and display the document. When you visit a website like Google.com, this is what actually takes place; your computer downloads a bunch of HTML code that looks like this:

```
<!doctype html><html itemscope="" itemtype="http://schema.org/WebPage" lang="en"><head><meta
content="Search the world's information, including webpages, images, videos and more. Google
has many special features to help you find exactly what you're looking for."
name="description"><meta content="noodp" name="robots"><meta
content="/logos/doodles/2018/celebrating-james-wong-howe-5981428998209536-l.png"
itemprop="image"><link href="/images/branding/product/ico/googleg_lodp.ico" rel="shortcut
icon"><meta content="Celebrating James Wong Howe" property="twitter:title"><meta
content="Celebrating James Wong Howe #GoogleDoodle" property="twitter:description"><meta
content="Celebrating James Wong Howe #GoogleDoodle" property="og:description"><meta
content="summary_large_image" property="twitter:card"><meta content="@GoogleDoodles"
property="twitter:site"><meta content="https://www.google.com/logos/doodles/2018/celebrating-
james-wong-howe-5981428998209536-2x.jpg" property="twitter:image"><meta
```

The above is the actual code taken from Google.com, it goes on for over 1000 lines. Your computer reads this code, interprets it, and displays the results. The result is that you see the Google homepage.

The program that fetches the code and displays the webpage for you is called a "web browser". Popular web browsers include Google Chrome, Mozilla Firefox, Microsoft Edge and Apple Safari. Below is an artistic rendition of what a web browser looks like, with the Google homepage opened inside it:

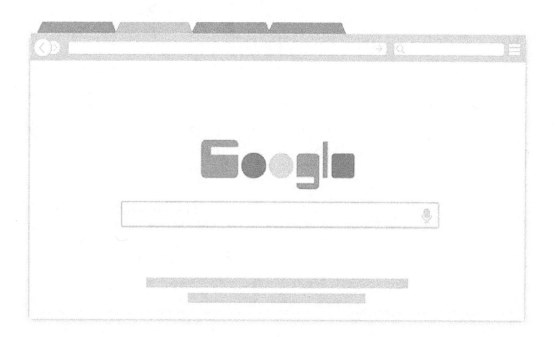

The browser is the thing with the tabs, back and forward buttons and address bar. It is a program that displays webpages for you, and it also interprets and runs JavaScript code as we will see.

To create a webpage on your computer, first open the Notepad program (for example by typing "Notepad" in the Start menu) (on a Mac, you would open TextEdit). Inside Notepad, write the following:

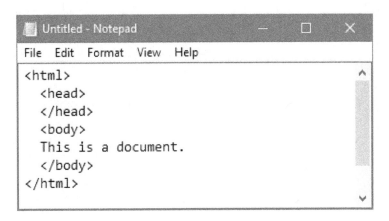

Above, we have written the definition for a barebones webpage. The spacing and indentation do not matter, you can write the above code all on one line.

Whenever you open a website on your computer, you are actually viewing a webpage transmitted from the website's computer to your computer. There is no need to worry about what **<html>**, **<head>**, etc. means right now.

After writing the above inside Notepad, go to **File -> Save**. Type anything you want as the file name, but end it with **.html**. This tells the computer you are making a webpage. Below I have chosen "**my_first_web_page.html**" as my file name.

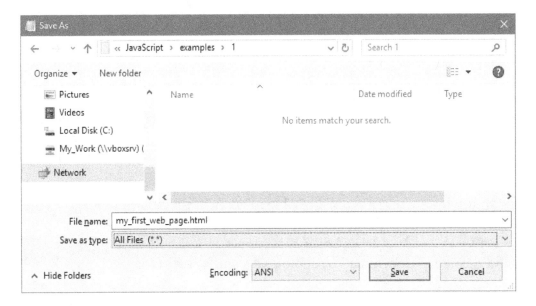

Once you have finished saving the file, you will see something like the following if you look inside the folder where you saved the file:

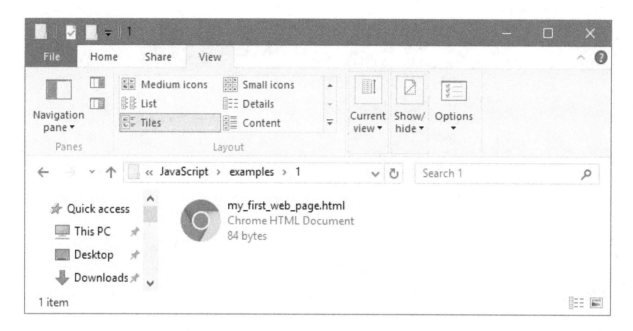

The file's icon will be different depending on your system. This does not make a difference for our purposes. Now, double-click the file to open it. Here is what shows up on my computer:

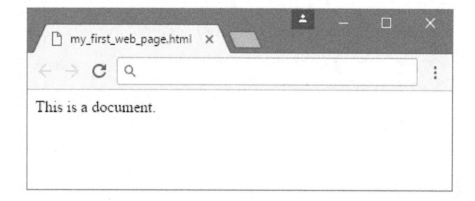

We have now created a webpage. If you put this file on a "server" (a type of computer connected to the Internet), people will be able to access it on the Internet.

Using the power of HTML, we can now make visual changes to the document. For example we can bold the word "document" by adding **** and **** before and after the word:

```
my_first_web_page.html - Notepad                    —    □    X
File  Edit  Format  View  Help
<html>
  <head>
  </head>
  <body>
  This is a <b>document</b>.
  </body>
</html>
```

If we now open the webpage again in a browser, this is what we will see:

```
my_first_web_page.html    X

←  →  C   Q

This is a document.
```

Below, I have changed the webpage in Notepad by adding two paragraphs to it, the first one has a black border around it:

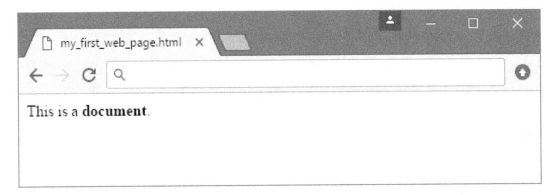

```
my_first_web_page.html - Notepad                    —    □    X
File  Edit  Format  View  Help
<html>
  <head>
  </head>
  <body>
  <p style="border:1px solid;">This is a paragraph.</p>
  <p>This is another paragraph.</p>
  </body>
</html>
```

Here is the result:

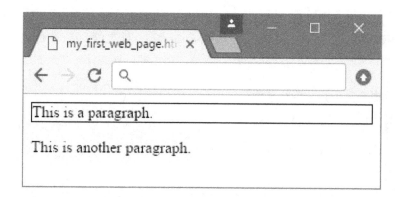

It is not the purpose of this book to teach HTML, I am merely giving you a glimpse of what it looks like. We will now start adding JavaScript to the webpage. Open the file again inside Notepad (open Notepad, then choose **File -> Open**) and add the following three lines to it (starting with **<script>** and ending with **</script>**):

```
my_first_web_page.html - Notepad

File  Edit  Format  View  Help

<html>
  <head>
    <script>
      alert('Hello there, person!');
    </script>
  </head>
  <body>
  This is a document.
  </body>
</html>
```

Make sure to type the single quotation marks before Hello and after the exclamation mark (the semicolon is not strictly necessary in this specific example). Save the file again and open it again in a browser, and this is what now happens:

As soon as you open the webpage, a dialog box opens. What you are seeing above is a JavaScript "alert", which is used to notify users about certain things. We have now officially done some JavaScript programming. In the HTML code, everything that goes between **<script>** and **</script>** is JavaScript code. Let's look at it again:

```
<script>
  alert('Hello there, person!');
</script>
```

We have two computer languages interacting with each other here. The first one is HTML, as we discussed. But inside the document, we use **<script>** to tell the computer that everything from there on is JavaScript, then use **</script>**) (note the slash) to tell the computer the JavaScript ends here and the HTML starts again after it.

We have a single line of JavaScript in the above example:

alert('Hello there, person!');

This line tells the computer to show an alert to the user when the user opens the file. If this webpage was placed on a website, any user visiting the site will have seen this alert. If the people at Google put this line of code in the JavaScript section of Google.com, everyone opening the Google homepage would have been shown such an alert.

And this is what coding or programming is. By writing a special piece of code (in the above example, by writing **alert('Hello there, person!')**), you command the computer to do a specific thing that you want it to do.

There is no need to worry about memorizing any of the code in this chapter. I am merely showcasing parts of JavaScript for you so that you can get a general feel for the way the language is used.

Let's now see another example. What if you wanted your webpage to show what the square root of 555 is? Below, I have removed the **alert...** inside the JavaScript and changed it as follows:

```
<script>
  document.write(Math.sqrt(555));
</script>
```

The above JavaScript tells the computer: "When a person opens this webpage, write out the square root of 555 at the beginning of the document". If we now open the webpage, this is what we see:

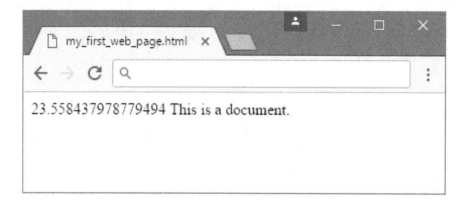

We used a multi-layered JavaScript command (or more correctly, JavaScript "statement") to tell the computer what to do. The **document.write()** command tells the computer: Write out anything you see between the brackets. We could have written **document.write('Hello!')** instead, as follows:

```
<script>
  document.write('Hello!');
</script>
```

And the result would have been as follows:

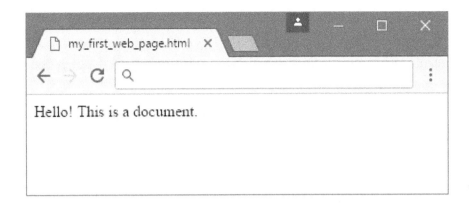

That is not very useful, since we can write a Hello! Without using any JavaScript. But by writing **document.write(Math.sqrt(555))** we use JavaScript's mathematical powers to do a complicated calculation behind the scenes and show people the result inside the webpage when they view it inside a browser. When the browser sees this line of JavaScript code, it knows that what we want is for it to calculate the square root of 555, then to write out the result inside the document. Since we did not tell the computer how to display the results, it showed us the square root of 555 with 15 decimals: **23.558437978779494**, which is a rather unnecessary level of detail. Computers have no common sense, so if we want them to do things a certain way, we have to spell it out for them. For example, we can use JavaScript's mathematical rounding powers to tell the computer to display the result in a more sensible way:

```
<script>
    document.write(Math.sqrt(555).toFixed(2));
</script>
```

Now, if we save the document and reload the webpage:

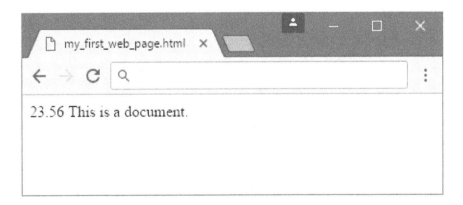

The JavaScript we are using (**document.write(Math.sqrt(555).toFixed(2));**) tells the computer to perform three actions one after the other. The first action is **Math.sqrt(555)**, which tells the computer to find out the square root of 555. The next action is **toFixed(2)**, which tells the computer to round the result of the previous action to two decimal places. The final action is **document.write()**, which tells the computer to write out the result inside the document. Without **document.write()**, the computer still performs the calculations, but it will not show the result:

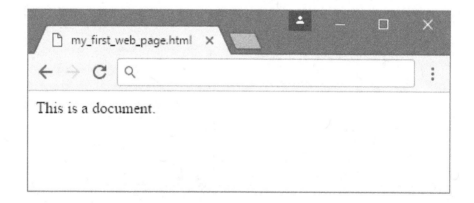

Here is the result:

That is quite useless, which is why we have to use some method of *outputting* the result of the calculation. To "output" something means to show users the result of some computer action. Without output, things may happen behind the scenes, but a person viewing the webpage will not be shown anything interesting. This is sometimes useful, for example companies like Google and Facebook use JavaScript to store information about you behind the scenes and send it back to their own computers. They then sell this information to advertisers. Usually when you visit any major website, thousands of lines of JavaScript run behind the scenes, doing all kinds of things that you do not see.

Back to our webpage, instead of using **document.write()**, we can use the **alert()** command that we showed earlier:

```
<script>
  alert(Math.sqrt(555).toFixed(2));
</script>
```

Now, if we reload the webpage:

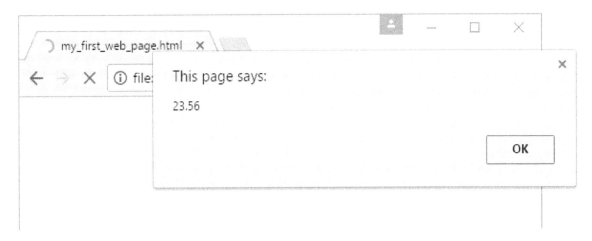

Above, a dialog box opens up that shows the result of **Math.sqrt(555).toFixed(2)**. If the user clicks **OK**, the dialog box closes and they will then see the document in its normal state:

We can show multiple alerts to users. For example:

```
<script>
  alert('Hello!');
  alert('Hello again!');
</script>
```

Now, if we reload the webpage, this is what happens:

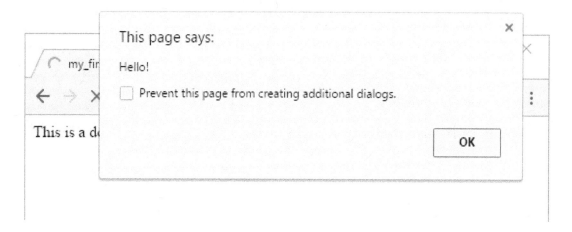

If we press **OK**, we are shown the second alert:

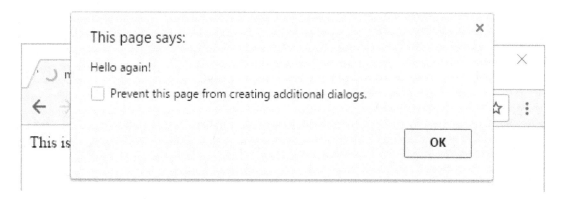

By using multiple alerts website owners can cause serious annoyances to their users, for this reason web browsers such as Google Chrome allow the user to stop the alerts from showing up for that particular web page by ticking the checkbox that says "Prevent this page…", which is what you are seeing above.

Tinkering with JavaScript using JS Tinker

We can continue doing JavaScript by changing the webpage in Notepad then opening it again in a browser. But this can get tiresome. For this reason we will use a free learning environment known as JS Tinker to learn programming. This is a web-based program that can be accessed at various websites (just do a web search for "js tinker"), including my personal website.[1] The program works inside the browser, there is no need to download or

---

[1] http://hawramani.com/wp-content/jstinker/index.html

install anything. There are also other similar programs like JS Fiddle[2] and CodePen[3] that one can use.

Below is a screenshot of the JS Tinker program:

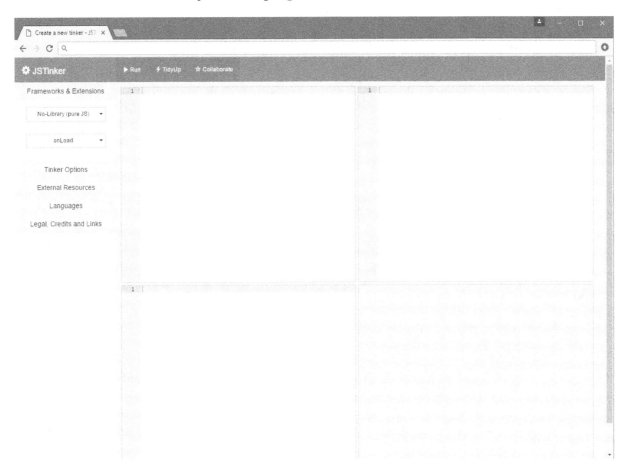

The program shows us four rectangular boxes. The top-left box is for HTML, the top right box for CSS (a language that we will not be using), and the bottom left is for JavaScript. The bottom right box displays the results. To clarify further, I will put a previous example inside the program:

---

[2] jsfiddle.net
[3] codepen.io

```
i  1 ▾ <html>
   2 ▾   <head>
   3 ▾     <script>
   4           document.write('Hello!');
   5         </script>
   6       </head>
   7 ▾   <body>
   8     This is a document
   9     </body>
  10   </html>
  11
  12   |
```

Hello! This is a document

Above, the numbers you see on the left of the HTML box are added by JS Tinker and are not part of the code. They are merely there to help you know the line number of each line, which can be helpful when coding.

Above, I put the previous code in the HTML box, clicked the "Run" button at the top of the program, and this caused the program to print out the result in the bottom-right box. JS Tinker does the job of interpreting the HTML and JavaScript for us and displays the results. This helps us avoid the need of having to save the code in a file and open it again every time we want to make a change. We can change anything we want and click "Run" to immediately see the result.

Instead of having the JavaScript in the HTML box, we can move it to the JavaScript box as follows:

```
i  1 ▾ <html>
   2 ▾   <head>
   3       </head>
   4 ▾   <body>
   5     This is a document
   6     </body>
   7   </html>
   8
   9   |
```

```
⚠ 1   document.write('Hello!');
   2   |
```

Hello!

JS Tinker automatically merges the HTML and the JavaScript and displays the result. Due to the way that JS Tinker works, this merging causes **document.write()** to overwrite the entire contents of the document, which is why we no longer see "This is a document". This issue will be clarified later.

2. Outputs and Variables

Check out the HTML code below:

```
i  1▾  <html>
   2▾    <head>
   3      </head>
   4▾    <body>
   5        The word 'king' is made up of x letters
   6      </body>
   7    </html>
   8
   9  |
```

The word 'king' is made up of x letters

I have changed the JS Tinker program to only show the HTML box and the output box since that takes up less space for the purposes of this book. We will now replace the "x" on line 5 with some JavaScript that actually calculates the length of the word and prints it out:

```
i  1▾  <html>
   2▾    <head>
   3      </head>
   4▾    <body>
   5▾      The word 'king' is made up of <script>
   6            document.write('king'.length);
   7        </script> letters
   8      </body>
   9    </html>
```

The word 'king' is made up of 4 letters

We injected some JavaScript into the sentence to make it dynamically print out the length of the word "king". We can separate out the JavaScript from the rest of the text as follows. This does not affect the result:

```
i   1 ▾ <html>
    2 ▾   <head>
    3     </head>
    4 ▾   <body>
    5       The word 'king' is made up of
    6 ▾     <script>
    7           document.write('king'.length);
    8       </script>
    9       letters
   10     </body>
   11   </html>
```

The word 'king' is made up of 4 letters

HTML ignores line breaks, regardless of how many blank lines we add, the result remains the same:

```
i   1 ▾ <html>
    2 ▾   <head>
    3     </head>
    4 ▾   <body>
    5       The word 'king' is made up of
    6
    7
    8 ▾     <script>
    9           document.write('king'.length);
   10       </script>
   11
   12
   13       letters
   14     </body>
   15   </html>
```

The word 'king' is made up of 4 letters

This is useful for us since it allows us to add JavaScript anywhere we like without worrying about breaking apart sentences and paragraphs. If we *did* want to add line breaks, we can always use tags like **
** in our HTML.

The JavaScript we used to calculate the length of the word king is as follows:

$$\texttt{document.write('king'.length);}$$

Above, it does not matter whether you put "king" in single quotes or double quotes. But it must be in quotes.

The **document.write()** part, as you may recall, simply tells the browser to print out whatever is between the brackets. The interesting part of the code is **'king'.length**. If we remove the **.length** part, here is the result:

```
i   1 ▾ <html>
    2 ▾   <head>
    3     </head>
    4 ▾   <body>
    5       The word 'king' is made up of
    6 ▾     <script>
    7           document.write('king');
    8       </script>
    9       letters
   10     </body>
   11   </html>
```

The word 'king' is made up of king letters

Above, the JavaScript merely prints out the word "king". By using `.length` after `'king'` (without any spaces), we are telling the browser that we are not interested in the word "king" itself, we are only interested in its length. It literally means: 'Access the "length" property of "king"'. When the computer does that, the result is 4, because the `.length` property, unsurprisingly, counts the length of the thing that comes before it. Since "king" is made up of 4 letters, its `.length` property is 4.

We should now clarify something. The JavaScript has no relationship with HTML outside of it. For example if in the HTML I change the word "king" to "elephant", the JavaScript will continue thinking about the word "king":

```
 i    1 ▾  <html>
      2 ▾    <head>
      3       </head>
      4 ▾    <body>
      5         The word 'elephant' is made up of
      6 ▾      <script>
      7           document.write('king'.length);
      8         </script>
      9         letters
     10       </body>
     11    </html>
```

The word 'elephant' is made up of 4 letters

Above, the JavaScript code continues to count the length of "king", because that is what we are telling it to do. The command **document.write('king'.length);** has a very specific meaning and has nothing to do with whatever might be outside the JavaScript.

To correct things, we have to change the word "king" to "elephant" inside the JavaScript too (line 7 below):

```
 i    1 ▾  <html>
      2 ▾    <head>
      3       </head>
      4 ▾    <body>
      5         The word 'elephant' is made up of
      6 ▾      <script>
      7           document.write('elephant'.length);
      8         </script>
      9         letters
     10       </body>
     11    </html>
```

The word 'elephant' is made up of 8 letters

What if there was a way to write the word "elephant" only once, so that we could avoid having to update the JavaScript every time we update the HTML? In fact we can do that by using JavaScript.

```
 i  1 ▾ <html>
    2 ▾   <head>
    3       </head>
    4 ▾   <body>
    5 ▾     The word '<script>
    6             document.write('elephant');
    7       </script>' is made up of
    8 ▾     <script>
    9             document.write('elephant'.length);
   10       </script>
   11       letters
   12     </body>
   13   </html>
```

The word 'elephant' is made up of 8 letters

Above, we are using JavaScript in two places. First we use it to print out the word "elephant" (line 6), then we used to print out the length of the word "elephant" (line 9). This so far hasn't solved the problem, if you change the word "elephant" on line 6, line 9 will continue to print out the length of the word "elephant". What we will do is use a *variable* to store the word we are interested in, then we will use the variable where we need to.

```
 i  1 ▾ <html>
    2 ▾   <head>
    3       </head>
    4 ▾   <body>
    5 ▾     The word '<script>
    6             var my_word = 'elephant';
    7             document.write(my_word);
    8       </script>' is made up of
    9 ▾     <script>
   10             document.write(my_word.length);
   11       </script>
   12       letters
   13     </body>
   14   </html>
```

The word 'elephant' is made up of 8 letters

Above, on line 6, I declared a variable called **my_word**. A variable acts as a container or box that you can put stuff inside so that you can access it later on. On line 6, I declare that the browser should create a variable named **my_word**, and that inside it there should be the word 'elephant'.

Let's now look at line 6 closely:

var my_word = 'elephant';

In JavaScript, we declare variables using the keyword **var**. This tells the computer that we are making a new variable. The name we choose for the variable can be anything, it is merely a label. On line 7, we declare that the contents of the variable **my_word** should be printed out. The JavaScript command **document.write()** doe looks inside the container that we have named **my_word** and prints out its contents on the screen. Since on line 6 we placed the word 'elephant' inside the variable, on line 7 **document.write()** ends up bringing out the word 'elephant'.

But things do not stop there. On line 10, we declare that the length of the variable my_word should be printed out, and since **my_word** contains the word "elephant", what ends up happening is that JavaScript prints out the length of the word 'elephant'.

We can now change the word "elephant" to anything we want and JavaScript will correctly print out its length:

```
i  1 ▾ <html>
   2 ▾   <head>
   3     </head>
   4 ▾   <body>
   5 ▾     The word '<script>
   6           var my_word = 'xylophone';
   7           document.write(my_word);
   8         </script>' is made up of
   9 ▾     <script>
  10           document.write(my_word.length);
  11         </script>
  12         letters
  13       </body>
  14   </html>
```

The word 'xylophone' is made up of 9 letters

Note the semicolons we have placed at the end of every line of JavaScript. The semicolon declares that the JavaScript instruction right before it has ended. Without it, the computer thinks that the stuff on the next line is still a continuation of the same instruction, which causes the JavaScript to stop working correctly. JS Tinker is a smart program that automatically corrects some mistakes, therefore even if you leave out a semicolon things will often continue functioning normally. But in real-world JavaScript forgetting the semicolon can cause your JavaScript to stop working.

We may put multiple JavaScript instructions on the same line, as follows:

```
   4 ▾   <body>
   5 ▾     The word '<script>
   6           var my_word = 'xylophone'; document.write(my_word);
   7         </script>' is made up of
   8 ▾     <script>
   9           document.write(my_word.length);
  10         </script>
  11         letters
  12       </body>
```

Above, I have merged the earlier lines 6 and 7 onto a single line 6. We can put any number of instructions on the same line as long as they are separated by semicolons. Here we can see the importance of semicolons. Below, I have removed the semicolon after 'xylophone':

```
i  1 ▾ <html>
   2 ▾   <head>
   3     </head>
   4 ▾   <body>
   5 ▾     The word '<script>
   6           var my_word = 'xylophone' document.write(my_word);
   7         </script>' is made up of
```

The word " is made up of 9 letters

23

The result is that the **document.write()** instruction that comes after it ends up doing nothing, so that the variable is not printed out (in the preview area on the right, see the way the word "xylophone" no longer appears).

As already mentioned, we can name our variables anything we want:

```
i   1▾ <html>
    2▾   <head>
    3     </head>
    4▾   <body>
    5▾     The word '<script>
    6            var interesting_word = 'xylophone';
    7            document.write(interesting_word);
    8         </script>' is made up of
    9▾      <script>
   10            document.write(interesting_word.length);
   11         </script>
   12         letters
```

The word 'xylophone' is made up of 9 letters

Above, I have changed the variable name from **my_word** to **interesting_word**. It does not affect the result of the code.

We can declare multiple variables in JavaScript with a single statement (in JavaScript a statement is anything that ends in a semicolon. Above I referred to statements as instructions, since statements *are* instructions to the computer. But the word "statement" is the correct technical term).

```
<script>
    var cat_sound = 'meow',
        dog_sound = 'bark';
</script>
```

In the above code block, we declare two variables, **cat_sound** and **dog_sound**. Notice that at the end of the line for the sound of cats, we do not have a semicolon but a comma. This tells JavaScript that we have another variable to declare. Once we are done declaring all of our variables, we use the semicolon.

The above code block is the same as the following in its meaning:

```
<script>
    var cat_sound = 'meow';
    var dog_sound = 'bark';
</script>
```

Above, we use two separate statements, each of them ending in a semicolon. It is a matter of preference which one you use. The earlier method requires less typing since you have to type **var** only once.

Below we go about making use of the variables:

```
i   1 ▾  <html>
    2 ▾    <head>
    3      </head>
    4 ▾    <body>
    5 ▾      <script>
    6            var cat_sound = 'meow',
    7                dog_sound = 'bark';
    8        </script>
    9        Cats
   10        <script>document.write(cat_sound);</script>
   11        and dogs
   12        <script>document.write(dog_sound);</script>.
   13      </body>
   14   </html>
```

Cats meow and dogs bark.

Above, we use three separate JavaScript code blocks. In the first one, we merely declare the variables without doing anything with them. We use HTML to print out the word "Cats", then the JavaScript code block prints out the value of the **cat_sound** variable. The same is done for the dog sound.

If we write out the same JavaScript statement multiple times, it will be carried out multiple times, as follows:

```
i   1 ▾  <html>
    2 ▾    <head>
    3      </head>
    4 ▾    <body>
    5 ▾      <script>
    6            var cat_sound = 'meow',
    7                dog_sound = 'bark';
    8        </script>
    9        Cats
   10 ▾      <script>
   11            document.write(cat_sound);
   12            document.write(cat_sound);
   13            document.write(cat_sound);
   14        </script>
   15        and dogs
   16        <script>document.write(dog_sound);</script>.
   17      </body>
   18   </html>
```

Cats meowmeowmeow and dogs bark.

Above, on lines 11-13 we have the same statement printing out the cat sound, so that on right-hand side we see "meowmeowmeow" being printed out. There are no spaces between the "meow"'s because we have not told JavaScript to put spaces between them. We can do so as follows:

```
i  1▾ <html>
   2▾   <head>
   3     </head>
   4▾   <body>
   5▾     <script>
   6          var cat_sound = 'meow',
   7              dog_sound = 'bark';
   8      </script>
   9      Cats
  10▾     <script>
  11        document.write(cat_sound);
  12        document.write(' ');
  13        document.write(cat_sound);
  14        document.write(' ');
  15        document.write(cat_sound);
  16      </script>
  17      and dogs
```

Cats meow meow meow and dogs bark.

On lines 12 and 14, I have added the statements **document.write(' ');**. The stuff inside **document.write()** may look strange, but it is merely a space with single quotes on each side of it. It is telling JavaScript to print out a space.

We can accomplish the same effect by using a single **document.write()** command through the use of *concatenation*, as follows on line 11:

```
i  1▾ <html>
   2▾   <head>
   3     </head>
   4▾   <body>
   5▾     <script>
   6          var cat_sound = 'meow',
   7              dog_sound = 'bark';
   8      </script>
   9      Cats
  10▾     <script>
  11        document.write(cat_sound + ' ' + cat_sound + ' ' + cat_sound);
  12      </script>
  13      and dogs
  14      <script>document.write(dog_sound);</script>.
  15    </body>
  16  </html>
```

Cats meow meow meow and dogs bark.

Above, on line 11 we are using the plus sign to combine different pieces of text together. We are combining a cat sound with a space, and combining that with another cat sound, with another space, with another cat sound, then printing out the result.

The plus sign is known as an "operator" in programming. It performs operations on the thing or things that are given to it.

Below we have a new example that we will use to showcase some more concatenation. On line 2 we declare a variable by the name of "**fruit**", then on line 3 we write out its contents. The result is that we see the word 'apple' on the little preview area on the right-hand side:

```
i  1▾ <script>
   2        var fruit = 'apple';
   3        document.write(fruit);
   4  </script>
   5  |
```

apple

Above, to simplify the code, I have only included the **<script>** tag. I skipped the **<html>**, **<head>** and **<body>** tags because they are not strictly necessary for our purposes. JS Tinker automatically adds them behind the scenes. The above example is the same as if we had typed out the following:

```
i  1▾ <html>
   2▾     <head>
   3      </head>
   4▾     <body>
   5▾       <script>
   6            var fruit = 'apple';
   7            document.write(fruit);
   8        </script>
   9      </body>
  10  </html>
```

apple

But the first example is shorter and takes up less space.

Below I have added a bit of additional code to the **document.write()** statement:

```
i  1▾ <script>
   2        var fruit = 'apple';
   3        document.write('the word ' + fruit);
   4  </script>
```

the word apple

On line 3, we have the text that says **'the word '** concatenated with the variable **fruit** using the **+** operator.

Below, I have placed an illustration of the way the above code works behind the scenes:

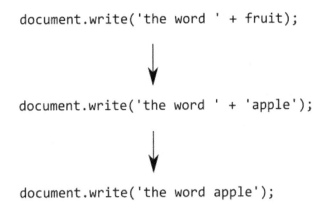

```
document.write('the word ' + fruit);

              ↓

document.write('the word ' + 'apple');

              ↓

document.write('the word apple');
```

At the second stage above, the variable **fruit** has been "evaluated" by the browser, meaning that its contents have been extracted in order to be used in an operation. The operation is concatenation, the result of which can be seen at the last stage.

Notice the way there is a space after "word" and before the single quotation mark in **'the word '**. That is necessary in order to show a space between "the word" and "apple" in the output. Here is what happens if we remove it:

```
i  1 ▾ <script>
   2       var fruit = 'apple';
   3       document.write('the word' + fruit);
   4   </script>
```
the wordapple

Above, "word" and "apple" merge together because we have not told JavaScript to create a space between them. We can add a space either by adding a space after "word", or as follows:

```
i  1 ▾ <script>
   2       var fruit = 'apple';
   3       document.write('the word' + ' ' + fruit);
   4   </script>
```
the word apple

Above, we are explicitly adding a space between the two bits of text. In many cases JavaScript ignores any space or new line inside the code, so if we separate out the stuff inside **document.write()** onto their own lines, this does not change anything:

```
i  1 ▾ <script>
   2       var fruit = 'apple';
   3       document.write(
   4           'the word'
   5           + ' '
   6           + fruit
   7       );
   8   </script>
```
the word apple

Above, the closing bracket for **document.write()** has been pushed all the way down to line 7. Any text you wish to print out must be enclosed in quotation marks, otherwise JavaScript will think that it is a JavaScript instruction. Below I have added the word "is" on line 7, but I have neglected to add the quotation marks:

```
i  1▾ <script>
   2      var fruit = 'apple';
   3      document.write(
   4          'the word'
   5          + ' '
   6          + fruit
   7          + is
   8      );
   9  </script>
```

We see no output in the preview area because the code has stopped working. JavaScript thinks we are trying to access a variable named **is**, which does not exist, so it makes the code crash.

Below, I have corrected the code by adding quotation marks around "is":

```
i  1▾ <script>
   2      var fruit = 'apple';
   3      document.write(
   4          'the word'
   5          + ' '
   6          + fruit
   7          + 'is'
   8      );
   9  </script>
```
the word appleis

Now the code is working, except that the word "apple" and "is" are merged together. This is something that you will run into time and again when concatenating text. To correct it, below I have added a space before "is", but *inside* the quotation mark:

```
i  1▾ <script>
   2      var fruit = 'apple';
   3      document.write(
   4          'the word'
   5          + ' '
   6          + fruit
   7          + ' is'
   8      );
   9  </script>
```
the word apple is

Adding spaces outside the quotation mark has no effect, as follows on line 7:

```
i  1▾ <script>
   2      var fruit = 'apple';
   3      document.write(
   4          'the word'
   5          + ' '
   6          + fruit
   7          +     'is'
   8      );
   9  </script>
```
the word appleis

The reason is that, as has been mentioned, JavaScript ignores spaces inside its code, *unless* the space is part of a piece of text enclosed in quotation marks.

Below we have added some additional detail to our code:

```
 1  <script>
 2      var fruit = 'apple';
 3      document.write(
 4          'the word'
 5          + ' '
 6          + fruit
 7          + ' is made up of '
 8          + fruit.length
 9          + ' letters.'
10      );
11  </script>
```

the word apple is made up of 5 letters.

On line 8, I use **fruit.length** to get the length of the contents of the variable **fruit**. Let's now talk about what **fruit.length** really means. As you now know, **fruit** is the name of a variable we declared on line 2. As for **length**, it is a *property* of the variable **fruit** that tells us how many letters the variable contains. The dot between them tells JavaScript that what comes after is a property of what comes before it.

Data types

In programming, we have various "data types" that we use for storing information. The main data types we run into are strings and numbers. We have already used strings. So far I have called them "text". A string in JavaScript is the stuff enclosed inside quotation marks, for example **'apple'** below:

```
 1  <script>
 2      var fruit = 'apple';
 3      var year = 2018;
 4  </script>
```

Above, on line 2, we have a string variable named **fruit**. It contains the string **'apple'**. We also have a number variable named **year**. It contains the number **2018**. Note the way **2018** does not have quotation marks around it.

We have different data types in programming because some things only make sense when applied to strings, other things only when applied to numbers. The way the computer stores one data type behind the scenes is completely different from the way it stores another data type, and this can make all the difference in the world in the way a program works and how fast it runs.

Below we have an example of a bit of nonsense, we are trying to divide a string by 2018:

```
i 1▾ <script>
  2        var fruit = 'apple';
  3        var year = 2018;
  4        document.write(fruit / year);
  5    </script>
```

NaN

When we try to divide **'apple'** by **2018** using the slash on line 4 inside **document.write()**, the result is **NaN** which means "not a number". When you see **NaN**, it means you are trying to do something that does not make sense in JavaScript.

In JavaScript, as seen above, the forward slash (/) is used for division. Below we divide the **year** variable by 2, resulting in 1009:

```
i 1▾ <script>
  2        var fruit = 'apple';
  3        var year = 2018;
  4        document.write(year / 2);
  5    </script>
```

1009

The length property we spoke of earlier only works on strings (and arrays and objects, which will be discussed later). It does not work on numbers:

```
i 1▾ <script>
  2        var fruit = 'apple';
  3        var year = 2018;
  4        document.write(year.length);
  5    </script>
```

undefined

Above I try to access a supposed **length** property of the **year** variable, but the result is **undefined**. The reason is that JavaScript does not have a **length** property for numbers, so when we try to access it, JavaScript tells us it is not defined.

In the following example, we have a string variable named **fruit** with the string **'apple'** inside it. We also have a number variable named **x** with the number **1000** inside it.

```
i 1▾ <script>
  2        var fruit = 'apple';
  3        var x = 1000;
  4        document.write(fruit + x);
  5    </script>
```

apple1000

Above, on line 4 we are concatenating the two variables. Unlike with division, this does not lead to an error. JavaScript converts the number to a string, then concatenates it with 'apple' to result in apple1000. It is the context that determines whether we will get an error or not. Dividing a string by a number does not make sense, so it results in an error. But adding a string to a number can be made to make sense. It is a little strange and can confuse people, but this is how JavaScript works. In other languages, such as C, you get an error if you try to add a string and a number. But languages like JavaScript try to be clever and guess what you were trying to do.

Below, I have added a new number variable on line 4 named **y** with the number **2000** inside it:

```
i 1 ▾ <script>
  2        var fruit = 'apple';
  3        var x = 1000;
  4        var y = 2000;
  5        document.write(x + y);
  6    </script>
```
3000

On line 5, I use the plus operator to add **x** and **y**. Since both of them are numbers, JavaScript performs mathematical addition, resulting in the number 3000, which is the sum of 1000 and 2000. It is the context that determines what the plus operator will do. If it is dealing with strings, it merges the strings together. If it is dealing with numbers, it performs addition. If it is dealing with a mix of strings and numbers, it merges them as if they are all strings.

Since both **x** and **y** are numbers, we can do division on them without this leading to an error, as follows on line 5:

```
i 1 ▾ <script>
  2        var fruit = 'apple';
  3        var x = 1000;
  4        var y = 2000;
  5        document.write(x / y);
  6    </script>
```
0.5

Below, on line 5, I have created a new variable named **result**. Instead of putting a number or string directly inside it, what I put inside is **x / y**. What this means is that JavaScript will perform this operation and then put the results inside the variable:

```
i 1 ▾ <script>
  2        var fruit = 'apple';
  3        var x = 1000;
  4        var y = 2000;
  5        var result = x / y;
  6        document.write(result);
  7    </script>
```
0.5

On line 6, I print out the contents of **result** , which as you might expect, is whatever we get when we divide the contents of **x** by **y** (0.5).

We can use the same variable multiple times in the same calculation. On line 5 below, we add **x** to **x**, then add that to **y**, resulting in the number 4000:

```
i  1 ▾ <script>
   2       var fruit = 'apple';
   3       var x = 1000;
   4       var y = 2000;
   5       var result = x + x + y;
   6       document.write(result);
   7  </script>
```
4000

Below, on line 5 I do the same calculation as the one above, but on line 6, in a new statement, I do a different calculation and assign the results to the **result** variable:

```
i  1 ▾ <script>
   2       var fruit = 'apple';
   3       var x = 1000;
   4       var y = 2000;
   5       var result = x + x + y;
   6       result = x + 1;
   7       document.write(result);
   8  </script>
```
1001

What happens is that on line 5 the **result** variable ends up containing the number 4000. But the next statement *overwrites* the variable, causing it to contain the result of **x + 1**.

Below, I overwrite the variable another time on line 7, causing it to become a string:

```
i  1 ▾ <script>
   2       var fruit = 'apple';
   3       var x = 1000;
   4       var y = 2000;
   5       var result = x + x + y;
   6       result = x + 1;
   7       result = 'banana';
   8       document.write(result);
   9  </script>
```
banana

JavaScript does not care that the **result** variable used to contain a number in the past. When we declare on line 7 that it should contain the string **'banana'**, that is what happens. The results of the previous calculations are discarded, and the **result** variable goes from being a number to a string.

Some languages do not let you do such a thing, if you try to put a number inside a variable that used to contain a string or vice versa, you will get an error. But in JavaScript you can do this. Languages that allow such a thing are known as *dynamically typed* languages; the data types are "dynamic", in one statement a variable might be a string, then the next operation might turn it into a number. Other languages use *static typing*, in such languages trying to put a string inside a number variable causes the program to crash.

Interpolation

The presence of a mix of strings and numbers causes JavaScript to make a guess about whether to treat everything as numbers or as strings. Let's take a look at the following:

```
1  <script>
2      document.write('a'  + 500 + 500);          a500500
3  </script>
```

Above, since the *first* operand in the operation is a string (the string **'a'**, JavaScript treats the entire operation as a string operation. It treats the numbers 500 and 500 as strings, instead of doing mathematical addition on them, it merely puts them side-by-side, performing string concatenation.

Below, we have reversed the order of the operation:

```
1  <script>
2      document.write(500 + 500 + 'a');           1000a
3  </script>
```

Strangely, JavaScript now performs mathematical addition on the numbers, resulting in the number 1000, then it performs concatenation. The reason is that in JavaScript the order of operations goes from left to right, the same as in mathematics. When JavaScript sees two numbers with a plus sign between them, it performs mathematical addition. When it sees a number and a string with a plus sign between them, it performs string concatenation. This can be an endless source of confusion, therefore good programmers do not write code like that above. They first make sure everything is a string or a number before using a plus sign between them. Later we will discuss how this is done.

The above discussion only applies to the plus sign. Since division, multiplication and subtraction are always mathematical, they are only allowed on numbers. For instance, let's look at the following:

```
1  <script>
2      document.write(500 * 500 * 'a');           NaN
3  </script>
```

Above, we are using the multiplication operator ***** to multiply 500 by 500 by the string **'a'**, which results in the **NaN** error. The same happens if we use the minus sign:

```
i 1▾ <script>
  2      document.write(500 - 500 - 'a');
  3   </script>
```
NaN

The same applies to division.

But if we multiply 500 by 500, then use the plus sign to add that to a string, things work, due to the fact that JavaScript performs operations from left to right one after another:

```
i 1▾ <script>
  2      document.write(500 * 500 + 'a');
  3   </script>
```
250000a

What happens above is that JavaScript sees two numbers being multiplied, so it performs mathematical multiplication. Next, it sees the number 25000 being added to the string **'a'**, so it switches gears and performs string concatenation.

Variable names

Programming languages have rules for what names you can use for variables. You can use lowercase, uppercase and number characters. You may also use underscores. These are all valid variable names:

my_variable
my_Variable
myVariable
MyVariable
MyVariable1
_my_variable

The last example above actually starts with an underscore. That is perfectly valid. However, the first important rule to remember is that you cannot have numbers at the beginning of a variable name, so the following JavaScript statement is invalid:

```
var 1st_name = 'James';
```

You may not use dashes (i.e. the minus sign), spaces and most special characters (such as the percentage sign) in variable names either. You can use dollar signs, however.

For now, to avoid errors in the code you try, keep using alphabetic letters and underscores to avoid errors.

Checking errors

The piece of code below has an error in it that prevents it from working. But what is the error?

```
1 ▼ <script>
2       document.write(Hello);
3 </script>
```

For a beginner to programming, it can be very difficult to find out why their code is not working. However, web browsers provide a useful "error console" that can sometimes help you find out what is wrong with your code. Below, there is a screenshot that shows how to access the error console in the Chrome web browser. In whatever browser you are using, go to the settings menu and find the "Developer tools" item (or something similar). In Chrome this option is actually hidden away, you have to click "More tools" first then you will see it:

Another way of accessing the error console is to right-click on a blank area of the page and click "Inspect" (the bottom menu item below):

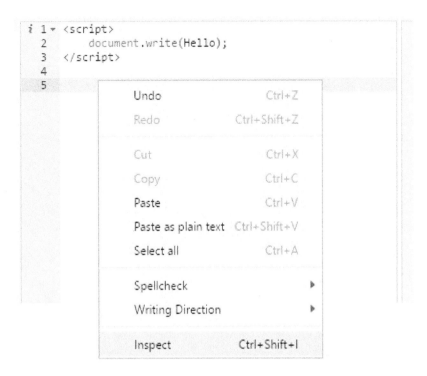

Once you do the above, the browser's developer tools are displayed (see the bottom part of the following screenshot), which can be a bit overwhelming at first:

In the developer tools, click the "Console" tab to view JavaScript errors and certain other errors:

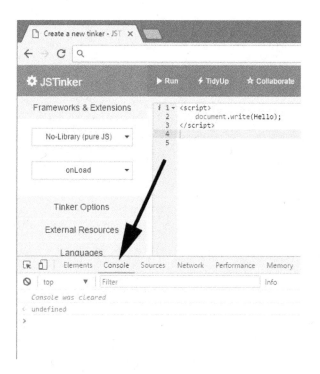

Now, if I click "Run" in JS Tinker to run the erroneous code shown earlier, here is what the console shows:

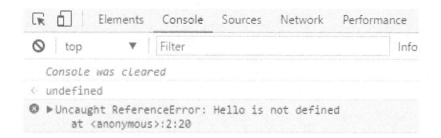

While the error messages that the console shows are not always very helpful (especially to beginners), when your code does not act as expected it can be helpful to take a look at the console. Above, the important part of the error message is "Hello is not defined". This tells us that JavaScript was trying to access a *variable* named **Hello** but failed because the variable was not declared. Let's take a look at the bad code again:

```
1 ▾ <script>
2       document.write(Hello);
3   </script>
4   |
5
```

In this simple piece of code, we are not dealing with any variables, so what is the console talking about? The problem with the code is that we forgot to put quotation marks before and after the word "Hello", so JavaScript thinks **Hello** is a variable name. To correct the problem, below I have added the necessary quotation marks:

```
i 1 ▾ <script>
  2       document.write('Hello');
  3   </script>
```

Hello

Now the code is working without issue.

Below we have a different example of erroneous code:

```
i 1 ▾ <script>
  2       var 1st_name = 'James';
  3   </script>
```

When running the above code, this is what the console tells us:

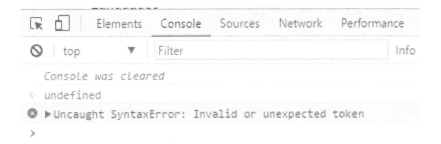

The error this time is "Invalid or unexpected token", which is a generic error message that tells us we have written nonsensical or bad JavaScript. In the above case, the issue is that the variable name **1st_name** starts with a number, which is not allowed.

By now, you have a reasonably good understanding of what a variable is and what strings are. If the rest of the discussion has left you a little bit confused or overwhelmed, there is no need to worry. You will see these concepts many more times in the next few chapters. You do not learn programming by memorizing things, but by running into the same concepts and tinkering with them over and over again in different settings.

3. Repeated Action

The most important benefit of computers is their ability to perform the same action over and over again. A computer can find the sum of a million numbers in a few seconds, something that would have required a human many days of work.

In programming, we have many ways of telling the computer to perform some action a certain number of times, or to continuously perform it until it reaches some result or condition. Starting from the simplest examples, we will slowly learn how to build complex algorithms. Below, we have the word "hellow" inside the variable named **the_word**. Notice how in the preview area on the right we see nothing. That is because we do not have any **document.write()** statements telling the computer to output stuff.

```
i  1▾ <script>
   2      var the_word = 'hello';
   3  </script>
```

Now, imagine if for some strange reason your boss asked you to create a document with the word "hello" written in it 1000 times. Instead of spending half an hour typing or copying and pasting, you can do it in a few seconds by writing a bit of JavaScript. We have already seen that we can do the same thing over and over again by repeatedly writing the same statement, as follows:

```
i  1▾ <script>                                    hellohellohello
   2      var the_word = 'hello';
   3      document.write(the_word);
   4      document.write(the_word);
   5      document.write(the_word);
   6  </script>
```

But writing or copying the JavaScript statement **document.write(the_word);** a thousand times is not the smartest way of achieving our goal. Instead, we will use a *loop*. A loop in programming is a piece of code that the computer runs over and over again. There are multiple type so loops in JavaScript. We will look at a *while loop* first:

```
1  <script>
2      var the_word = 'hello';
3      var number_of_hellos_printed_so_far = 0;
4      while(number_of_hellos_printed_so_far < 1000) {
5          document.write('hello');
6          number_of_hellos_printed_so_far =
7              number_of_hellos_printed_so_far + 1;
8      }
9  </script>
```

hellohellohellohello

Above, you see the complete code for writing out the word "hello" 1000 times. We will spend some time deconstructing it. In the preview areas we see the word "hello" four times. The text actually goes on, extending rightward, until 1000 "hello"s are printed, but there isn't sufficient space to show them all on this page.

In order to print exactly 1000 "hello"s, we need a way of keeping track of how many we have already printed. We do that using the **number_of_hellos_printed_so_far** variable declared on line 2. We first set it to zero, since on line 2 we have not printed anything so far. We next have the **while** loop. The basic structure of a while loop is as follows:

```
while(some_condition_is_true) {
    do something...
}
```

It basically tells the computer: As long as this condition applies, continually run the code below over and over again. The code that the **while** loop should run is enclosed in *curly braces*. These braces **{}** tell the **while** loop where it starts and where it ends.

In our example, the condition we have says that as long the value of the **number_of_hellos_printed_so_far** variable is less than 1000 (notice the mathematical "less than" symbol), the code inside the **while** loop should be repeatedly run over and over again.

When running a loop, what JavaScript does is that it carries out the statements inside the loop, then checks the condition again, then, if the condition is still true, it runs the code again.

Inside the **while** loop we have two statements. The first one (on line 5) prints out a "hello" using **document.write()**. The second statement, which takes up two lines (6 and 7) keeps track of how many "hello"s we have printed. I have broken a single statement into two lines only for readability's sake. This:

```
6          number_of_hellos_printed_so_far =
7            number_of_hellos_printed_so_far + 1;
```

is exactly the same as this:

```
number_of_hellos_printed_so_far = number_of_hellos_printed_so_far + 1;
```

We have line 7 slightly indented (it has slightly more spaces before it) to indicate to ourselves that this line continues from the one above it. The spaces do not do anything, they are merely for our reading benefit.

We keep track of how many "hello"s we have printed by updating the value of the **number_of_hellos_printed_so_far** variable. We add the number 1 to the value of the variable each time the loop runs. The very first time JavaScript runs the loop, the value of **number_of_hellos_printed_so_far** is zero as we declared on line 2. Then the statement on lines 6 and 7 add one to the value of the variable, so that the variable ends up containing the number 1. Once JavaScript finishes running one *iteration* of the loop (meaning running the code inside it once), it goes back to the top, checks the condition again, and if the condition is true, it then runs the code again. To refresh our memory, let's take another loop at the code for our while loop:

```
4 ▾    while(number_of_hellos_printed_so_far < 1000) {
5          document.write('hello');
6          number_of_hellos_printed_so_far
7            = number_of_hellos_printed_so_far + 1;
8      }
```

Below we have a textual description of what JavaScript is thinking as it runs the loop each time. The numbers at the beginning of each line represent the line number of the code above:

4 (start of while loop). Is the value of the variable number_of_hellos_printed_so_far less than 1000? Yes.

5. Print out a "hello".

6. Increase the value of number_of_hellos_printed_so_far by one. Go back to the top. (Now number_of_hellos_printed_so_far contains the number 1)

4. Is number_of_hellos_printed_so_far less than 1000? Yes.

5. Print out a "hello".

6. Increase the value of number_of_hellos_printed_so_far by one. Go back to the top. (Now number_of_hellos_printed_so_far contains the number 2)

4. Is number_of_hellos_printed_so_far less than 1000? Yes.

5. Print out a "hello".

6. Increase the value of number_of_hellos_printed_so_far by one. Go back to the top. (Now number_of_hellos_printed_so_far contains the number 3)

JavaScript will repeat the above thought process over and over again until it reaches the following, which represent the last two iterations of the loop:

4. Is number_of_hellos_printed_so_far less than 1000? Yes. (at this point number_of_hellos_printed_so_far has 999 inside it)

5. Print out a "hello".

6. Increase the value of number_of_hellos_printed_so_far by one. Go back to the top. (Now number_of_hellos_printed_so_far contains the number 1000)

4. Is number_of_hellos_printed_so_far less than 1000 now? No. Since the condition is now false, we cannot continue. This is the end of the loop.

In the very last iteration of the loop, the variable **number_of_hellos_printed_so_far** ends up containing 1000. When JavaScript next tries out the code **while(number_of_hellos_printed_so_far < 1000) {**, it compares the value of **number_of_hellos_printed_so_far** with 1000 to find out if it is less than it or not. Since **number_of_hellos_printed_so_far** contains 1000,

JavaScript is basically asking "Is 1000 less than 1000?". Of course it is not, which means that the *condition* for the loop is no longer true, which means the loop should no longer be run.

Infinite loops

The **while** loop runs only as long as its condition is true. The following piece of code will run *forever*:

```
i 1 ▾ <script>
  2 ▾     while(5 === 5) {
  3             document.write('hello');
  4         }
  5   </script>
```

Above, each time JavaScript prints out a "hello", behind the scenes it asks the question "Is 5 equal to 5?", and since the answer is always "Yes!", the loop keeps going without end. The weird three equal signs **===** between the two numbers is how we check for equality in JavaScript. Earlier we already saw how we check whether a variable is less than a certain number (using the mathematical "smaller than" sign, **<**). Here we are using the mathematical "is equal to" sign, which requires three equal signs in JavaScript for reasons that will become clear later on.

I recommend that you do not try out the code above because it creates what is known as an *infinite loop*, which can cause your browser to crash. An infinite loop is a loop whose condition is always true. It is similar to telling a robot, "Keep digging holes as long as water is wet".

Below is another infinite loop:

```
i 1 ▾ <script>
  2 ▾     while((1 + 1) === 2) {
  3             document.write('hello');
  4         }
  5   </script>
```

Above, we have told JavaScript to continuously print out "hello"s as long as adding the number one to one equals two. Since 1 + 1 will always equal 2, the loop will continue forever.

Below is an example of an infinite loop that involves strings and variables:

```
i  1 ▾ <script>
   2        var first_name = 'James';
   3 ▾      while(first_name === 'James') {
   4            document.write('Hello James!');
   5        }
   6    </script>
```

On line 3, we check whether or not the variable **first_name** contains the string **'James'**. Since this variable will always contain this string when JavaScript goes back to the top at the end of every iteration, the loop will go on forever.

Above, the single equal sign on line 2 tells JavaScript to place the string **'James'** inside the variable **first_name**. The triple equal sign on line 3 has a completely different and unrelated meaning. It is a comparison operator that checks whether the stuff on its left and right are exactly the same.

More while loops

Below we are trying to find out the result of continuously multiplying the number 500 by 2:

```
i  1 ▾ <script>                              16000
   2        var my_number = 500;
   3 ▾      while(my_number < 10000) {
   4            my_number = my_number * 2;
   5        }
   6        document.write(my_number);
   7    </script>
```

With each iteration of the loop, we multiply **my_number** by 2 on line 4 and store the new result inside the same variable. This overwrites the variable's previous value with the new one. On line 4, JavaScript calculates the result of **my_number * 2**, which is 1000 the first time the loop runs. It then puts this result inside the variable, so that once line 4 is finished running, **my_number** will contain the number 1000. The next time the loop runs, the same process repeats. JavaScript calculates the result of **my_number * 2**, which this time is 2000. Each iteration doubles the variable value.

On line 3, we have a condition in order to prevent an infinite loop. The condition tells JavaScript to run the loop as long as **my_number** is less than ten thousand.

On line 6, we print out the final value of **my_number** in the preview area, which is 16000. In order to find out why the end result is 16000, we can tell JavaScript to print out the value of **my_number** with every iteration of the loop:

```
i  1 ▾ <script>                                          500
   2       var my_number = 500;
   3 ▾     while(my_number < 10000) {                    1000
   4           document.write(my_number);                2000
   5           document.write('<br>');
   6           my_number = my_number * 2;                4000
   7       }                                             8000
   8       document.write(my_number);                    16000
   9  </script>
```

Above, every time the loop runs, on line 4 we print out the value of **my_number** which at first is 500 as seen at the top of the preview area. On line 5 we have something new. You do not need to understand what this line means, suffice it to say that it causes the next item to be printed on a new line. It basically means "start a new line at this point in the document". This is why the numbers are neatly stacked on each other; we are telling JavaScript to make a new line for each iteration of the loop.

On the next iterations of the loop, **my_number** ends up containing 1000, 2000, 4000 and 8000. On the final iteration, JavaScript checks whether 8000 is less than 10000 (on line 3). Since the answer is "Yes!", the loop continues to run. On line 4 the number 8000 is printed, then on line 6 the number is doubled by multiplying it by 2. JavaScript goes back to the top of the loop and asks, "Is 16000 less than 10000?", since this time the answer is "No!", the loop stops running. On line 8 we print out the final value of **my_number**, which is 16000, as seen at the bottom of the preview area.

The best way to learn programming is to read code and try to make sense of it. This is why I provide numerous examples in which similar concepts are treated. Many educational books overwhelm you with technical details and specifications and leave you to learn on your own. My teaching method is quite different from that. I help you see the same concepts in action in many different contexts, helping you get a natural feel for the way programming works.

4. Conditionals and Comparisons

In programming, we often have a need to check whether a variable is this way or that way before we perform a certain operation on it.

Below, we are trying to develop a little program for a shopping website that checks whether the user is allowed to buy cigarettes or not based on their age. If they are allowed, the site would let them add cigarettes to their shopping cart, otherwise it will not. We will not actually build the complete code for the whole website's shopping cart mechanism, since that requires very advanced code. We are simply looking at a very small section of such a website's code.

```
i  1 ▾ <script>
   2       var user_age = 28;
   3       var can_purchase_cigarettes = false;
   4 ▾     if(user_age >= 18) {
   5           can_purchase_cigarettes = true;
   6       }
   7   </script>
```

Above, on line 2 we declare a variable named **user_age** with the number 28 inside it. In a real program the user age will be dynamically retrieved from a database, but that is a topic for another day. Here we are manually setting it to 28 for the sake of the example.

On line 3, declare variable named **can_purchase_cigarettes** with the value **false** inside it. This variable is neither a string nor a number. It is a *boolean*. Boolean variables, named after the self-taught English mathematician George Boole (died 1864), can only contain the values **true** or **false**. Note how there are no quotation marks around the word **false** on line 3. If it had quotations, it would merely be a string variable with the word "false" inside it. But when we omit the quotation marks, we are declaring a boolean variable.

At this point in your learning it may seem strange that there is a whole type of variable dedicated to truth and falsehood, but as you progress, you will see that boolean variables are an essential part of programming.

On line 3, by declaring **can_purchase_cigarettes** false, we are assuming that no one can purchase cigarettes unless it can be proved that they can do so in the lines that follow. On line 4 we have and **if** statement. Similar to the **while** statement, the **if** takes a condition between brackets and has a bunch of code between its curly braces. As you know, JavaScript ignores whitespace, so below is a completely functional **if** statement:

```
if(1 < 2) { document.write('Yes!'); }
```

Above, we are telling JavaScript to print out a "Yes!" if one is less than two. Since one is truly less than two, when the code runs, "Yes!" will be printed out in the document. There is no need to have a semicolon at the end of the curly braces (at the very end of the line above), because in JavaScript *code blocks* do not need semicolons to tell JavaScript the block is finished. The presence of the closing curly brace is sufficient for JavaScript know that this block of code is done. A code block is the stuff in curly braces and can be made up of multiple lines of code as we have seen in the previous examples.

The while statement is designed to run a block of code a number of times. The if statement, on the other hand, is designed to run the block of code just once, and *only* if the condition is true. If the condition is false, the block of code is ignored and JavaScript goes on running anything else that follows afterwards.

Let's take another look at the example we were working on earlier:

```
i  1 ▾ <script>
   2      var user_age = 28;
   3      var can_purchase_cigarettes = false;
   4 ▾    if(user_age >= 18) {
   5          can_purchase_cigarettes = true;
   6      }
   7  </script>
```

On line 4, we are checking whether the **user_age** variable *is greater or equal to* 18. In JavaScript, **>=** means "greater or equal to". The greater sign has to be written first, then the equal sign (if you write **=>** , this has a completely different meaning and has nothing to do with comparison).

In the if statement's code block, we are setting the value of the **can_purchase_cigarettes** variable to **true** on line 5. Since this code runs *only* if the condition on line 4 is true, what this means is that this variable only gets set to **true** if the user's age is 18 or more.

Now we can add some output to our example:

```
i  1 ▾ <script>
   2        var user_age = 28;
   3        var can_purchase_cigarettes = false;
   4 ▾      if(user_age >= 18) {
   5            can_purchase_cigarettes = true;
   6        }
   7
   8 ▾      if(can_purchase_cigarettes === true) {
   9            document.write('Click here to '
  10            + 'view the cigarette section');
  11
  12        }
  13 ▾      else {
  14            document.write('Sorry, you cannot '
  15            + 'view the cigarette section');
  16        }
  17 </script>
```

Click here to view the cigarette section

Above, we have added a new section of code starting from line 8. In this section of code, we are telling JavaScript to print out "Click here to view the cigarette section", but *only if* the value of **can_purchase_cigarettes** is **true**. In the preview on the right, you see that the "Click here..." message was printed out. That is because on line 5 we set the value of **can_purchase_cigarettes** to **true**. Since the condition on line 8 is satisfied, the code underneath it runs. If you click on the message that says "Click here...", nothing actually happens right now since more code is needed to turn the message into something interactive. But we are not adding that code to keep the example simple.

On line 13 we have something new. It is an **else** statement. The **else** statement is the companion of the **if** statement. You do not always need it, but it is handy when you do need it. In the **else** statement's code block we write the code that we want to be executed when the **if** statement's condition is not satisfied. We are saying: If the user can purchase cigarettes then do this, but if not, do this other thing in the **else** section.

Above, the **else** statement does not do anything because the **if** statement's condition is true. We can make the **else** statement run by setting the **user_age** variable to something less than 18, such as 17:

```
i  1▾ <script>
   2      var user_age = 17;
   3      var can_purchase_cigarettes = false;
   4▾     if(user_age >= 18) {
   5          can_purchase_cigarettes = true;
   6      }
   7
   8▾     if(can_purchase_cigarettes === true) {
   9          document.write('Click here to '
  10          + 'view the cigarette section');
  11
  12      }
  13▾     else {
  14          document.write('Sorry, you cannot '
  15          + 'view the cigarette section');
  16      }
  17 </script>
```

Sorry, you cannot view the cigarette section

Above, the code is exactly the same as before except for line 2, where we declare that **user_age** is **17**. By changing line 2, we cause a whole cascade of effects on the rest of the program: The if statement on line 4 no longer runs since when JavaScript checks whether **user_age** is greater or equal to 18 behind the scenes, the answer is "No!". And this means that the code on line 5 is not executed, so that the value of **can_purchase_cigarettes** continues to be **false** because we declared it as **false** on line 3.

On line 8, we check if the variable **can_purchase_cigarettes** has the boolean value **true**. Since it does not, JavaScript ignores the **if** statement's code and jumps immediately to the **else** section. In the **else** section, we print out a message that tells the user they cannot view the cigarette section, and this is what we now see in the preview.

Multi-condition statements

We will now move on to a different example. In demographics, a country's "working age" population is defined as the population of people between the ages of 15 and 64. Below, we write a piece of code that decides whether someone is within the demographic working age or not based on their age.

```
 i   1 ▾  <script>
     2        var user_age = 17;
     3        var is_in_demographic_working_age = false;
     4
     5 ▾      if(user_age >= 15 && user_age <= 64) {
     6            is_in_demographic_working_age = true;
     7        }
     8
     9 ▾      if(is_in_demographic_working_age === true) {
    10            document.write('You are in the '
    11            + 'demographic working age.');
    12        }
    13
    14    </script>
```

You are in the demographic working age.

Above, the first two lines of code are simple. We have a variable with a person's age inside it, and another variable that keeps track of whether this person is within the demographic working age range or not. By default, we set this variable to **false**.

On line 5, we have an **if** statement with multiple conditions, which is something new. We have to check if the user's age is at least 15 *and* at most 64. The double ampersand (**&&**) in JavaScript is used to mean "and" in conditionals. We use it when we want to ensure that the condition on both left and right of it are both true at the same time. In our example, the first condition is **user_age >= 15**, which is true, since the age is 17, which is greater than 15. The second condition is **user_age <= 64**, (**<=** means "less than or equal to"), which is also true, since the **user_age** is 17, which is less than 64. On line 6 we set **is_in_demographic_working_age** to **true** if both conditions are met. In the next **if** statement on lines 9 to 12, we print out a message if the user is within the demographic working age.

Below, we expand our code to determine whether the user is in the *legal* working age or not, which is different from the demographic working age. The legal working age is differs according to the country. Here we will use the US federal working age, which is any age 16 or older.

```
i  1 ▾ <script>
   2       var user_age = 17;
   3       var is_in_demographic_working_age = false;
   4       var is_in_legal_working_age = false;
   5
   6 ▾     if(user_age >= 15 && user_age <= 64) {
   7           is_in_demographic_working_age = true;
   8       }
   9
  10 ▾     if(user_age >= 16) {
  11           is_in_legal_working_age = true;
  12       }
  13
  14 ▾     if(is_in_demographic_working_age === true) {
  15           document.write('You are in the '
  16           + 'demographic working age.');
  17       }
  18
  19 ▾     if(is_in_legal_working_age === true) {
  20           document.write('<br>');
  21           document.write('You are in the '
  22           + 'legal working age.');
  23       }
  24
  25   </script>
```

You are in the demographic working age.
You are in the legal working age.

Above, we have added a new variable on line 4 to keep track of whether the user is in the legal working age or not. We also have a new **if** statement on lines 10-12. This statement's condition is simpler than the one before it because we merely need to check if the age is greater or equal to 16. There is no maximum age to worry about. On lines 19-23, we print out a second line that tells the user they are in the legal working age if they truly are. On line 20 I used the statement introduced earlier in the book to print out a new line, so that the second message shows up on its own line.

Below, I have updated the part of the code that prints out messages. I have added **else** statements to tell the user they are not within each age range if they are not.

```
  14 ▾     if(is_in_demographic_working_age === true) {
  15           document.write('You are in the '
  16           + 'demographic working age.');
  17       }
  18 ▾     else {
  19           document.write('You are not in the '
  20           + 'demographic working age.');
  21       }
  22
  23 ▾     if(is_in_legal_working_age === true) {
  24           document.write('<br>');
  25           document.write('You are in the '
  26           + 'legal working age.');
  27       }
  28 ▾     else {
  29           document.write('<br>');
  30           document.write('You are not in the '
  31           + 'legal working age');
  32
  33       }
```

Below I have set the age to 15 on line 2:

```
i  1 ▾ <script>
   2       var user_age = 15;
   3       var is_in_demographic_working_age = false;
   4       var is_in_legal_working_age = false;
```

You are in the demographic working age.
You are not in the legal working age

The age 15 is in the demographic working age but not in the legal working age, so for the second message, it is message in the **else** section (lines 28-33) that shows up.

If I change the user's age to 70, the message switch up, because 70 is not in the demographic working age while it is in the legal working age since the legal working age has no limit:

```
i  1 ▾ <script>
   2       var user_age = 70;
   3       var is_in_demographic_working_age = false;
   4       var is_in_legal_working_age = false;
```

You are not in the demographic working age.
You are in the legal working age.

Brackets

In programming, as in mathematics, we can use brackets to ensure that things happen in a certain order.

```
i  1 ▾ <script>
   2       var x = 2 * 4 + 3;
   3       var y = (2 * 4) + 3;
   4       var z = 2 * (4 + 3);
   5       document.write('x is ' + x);
   6       document.write('<br>');
   7       document.write('y is ' + y);
   8       document.write('<br>');
   9       document.write('z is ' + z);
  10  </script>
```

x is 11
y is 11
z is 14

Above, we declare three variables and later print out their values. On lines 3 and 4 we add brackets into the calculation at different places. On line 3, we put **2 * 4** between brackets, telling JavaScript to perform this multiplication before adding the 3 at the end. Since this is what JavaScript would have done anyway whether we told it to or not, these brackets make no difference; the value of **x** and **y** is the same. On line 4, however, we add brackets between **4 + 3**. This makes a difference because now JavaScript carries out this addition operation before the multiplication. The result is that **z** ends up containing the number 14, since two times seven is fourteen.

"Or" conditions

We have already seen the double ampersand (**&&**) which is used to mean "and" in JavaScript conditionals. We also have the double pipe (**||**) which is used to mean "or". You type the pipe character by holding down Shift and pressing the backslash key on most keyboards.

In the following example, we have an imaginary school's website that parents, teachers and students can all user. The **user_type** variable keeps track of the type of user who is currently using the system. Sometimes there is a need to prevent students from seeing parts of the system that teachers and parents are allowed to see. Below, implement the logic of how this should be done:

```
 1   <script>
 2       var user_type = 'teacher';
 3
 4       if(user_type === 'teacher'
 5          || user_type === 'parent') {
 6       document.write('Stuff only '
 7       + 'parents and teachers '
 8       + 'can see...');
 9       }
10       else {
11           document.write('Sorry, '
12           + 'minors are not allowed '
13           + 'to view this section');
14       }
15   </script>
```

Stuff only parents and teachers can see...

Above, we have broken the **if** statement's condition onto two lines (lines 4 and 5) to make it take up less space in the screenshot. Lines 4 and 5 have the exact same meaning as this:

```
if(user_type === 'teacher' || user_type === 'parent') {
```

The if statement's condition says that if the user is a teacher or a parent, then do the stuff that follows. Since we declared the **user_type** as **'teacher'** on line 2, we see that the if statement runs and prints out the message "Stuff only parents and teachers can see…".

If we change the user's type to "parent" on line 2, the same message is still shown:

```
i  1▾ <script>
   2      var user_type = 'parent';
   3      if(user_type === 'teacher'
   4▾        || user_type === 'parent') {
   5        document.write('Stuff only '
   6        + 'parents and teachers '
   7        + 'can see...');
   8      }
   9▾     else {
  10          document.write('Sorry, '
  11          + 'minors are not allowed '
  12          + 'to view this section');
  13      }
  14  </script>
```

Stuff only parents and teachers can see...

When JavaScript evaluates (i.e. runs or executes) the condition in the **if** statement, it first checks the left side of the condition: **user_type === 'teacher'**. This condition fails, since the user type does not equal "teacher". Since we are using the double pipe between the two conditions, JavaScript evaluates the condition the right-hand side of the pipe: **user_type === 'parent'**. This condition does not fail, because the user type is indeed "parent". Therefore even though the first condition fails, since the second one succeeds, JavaScript executes the code inside the **if** statement's curly braces.

If we now change the user type to "student", the code of the **else** statement ends up running:

```
i  1▾ <script>
   2      var user_type = 'student';
   3      if(user_type === 'teacher'
   4▾        || user_type === 'parent') {
   5        document.write('Stuff only '
   6        + 'parents and teachers '
   7        + 'can see...');
   8      }
   9▾     else {
  10          document.write('Sorry, '
  11          + 'minors are not allowed '
  12          + 'to view this section');
  13      }
  14  </script>
```

Sorry, minors are not allowed to view this section

Now, we see the message "Sorry, minors are not allowed…".

Not equals

We have already seen that we can use the triple equal sign to check whether something is equal to something or not. We also have the "not equals" sign in programming:

```
i 1 ▾ <script>
  2      var number = 5;
  3 ▾    if(number !== 6) {
  4          document.write('The number is not six.');
  5      }
  6  </script>
```

The number is not six.

Above, we use JavaScript's "is not equal to" sign, which is an exclamation mark followed by two equal signs (**!==**) to check that **number** is not equal to 6. Since **number** contains the number 5, it really is not equal to six, therefore the condition is true and the code inside the **if** statement runs.

We often have multiple ways of achieving the same thing when programming. For example, below we rephrase the above code so that it no longer needs a "not equals" sign:

```
i 1 ▾ <script>
  2      var number = 5;
  3 ▾    if(number < 6 || number > 6) {
  4          document.write('The number is not six.');
  5      }
  6  </script>
```

The number is not six.

On line 3 above, we are saying that **number** should be either smaller than 6 or greater, which means that it should not be equal to six.

Mixed conditionals

We can mix the double pipe and double ampersand in the same conditional when necessary. Below we have an imaginary game where we have a warrior with certain powers. The warrior will be able to perform certain feats if certain conditions are true.

```
i 1 ▾ <script>
  2      var charisma = 5;
  3      var intelligence = 5;
  4      var strength = 10;
  5      var armor = 10;
  6      var can_defeat_dragon = false;
```

We have the variables **charisma**, **intelligence** and **strength** which keep track of the player's powers. In a real game these variables will change as the user progresses in the game. The **can_defeat_dragon** keeps track of whether the player has the power to defeat dragons or not. In this game, users can defeat dragons either by having high charisma and intelligence (so that they can outwit it), or by having very high strength and armor (so that they can defeat it in battle). We will now go about implementing these conditions in code:

```
i   1▾ <script>
    2       var charisma = 5;
    3       var intelligence = 5;
    4       var strength = 10;
    5       var armor = 10;
    6       var can_defeat_dragon = false;
    7
    8▾      if(charisma > 10 && intelligence > 10) {
    9           can_defeat_dragon = true;
   10       }
   11▾      if(armor > 100 && strength > 100) {
   12           can_defeat_dragon = true;
   13       }
   14
   15       document.write('Can you defeat a dragon? ');
   16
   17▾      if(can_defeat_dragon) {
   18           document.write('Yes');
   19       }
   20▾      else {
   21           document.write('No');
   22       }
   23  </script>
```

Can you defeat a dragon? No

In the **if** statement on lines 8-10, we set **can_defeat_dragon** to **true** if the player has both a **charisma** higher than 10 and an **intelligence** higher than 10. On lines 11-13, in a different if statement, we set **can_defeat_dragon** to **true** if the player has both an **armor** of 100 and **strength** of 100. Below that we have some output statements telling the user whether they can defeat dragons or not.

Now, if we increase both the **charisma** and the **intelligence** to 10 on lines 2 and 3, nothing changes:

```
i   1▾ <script>
    2       var charisma = 10;
    3       var intelligence = 10;
```

Can you defeat a dragon? No

That is because in the condition on line 8, we are requiring that the **charisma** and **intelligence** should be *more than 10*. This means that 10 is not enough, they have to be more. This is a common cause for programming errors, when programmers mistakenly write "greater than" when they mean "greater than or equal to". Below we increase the **charisma** and **intelligence** both to 11, which does satisfy the requirements for defeating dragons:

```
i   1▾ <script>
    2       var charisma = 11;
    3       var intelligence = 11;
```

Can you defeat a dragon? Yes

We can merge the two **if** statements on lines 8 to 13 into a single statement that accomplishes the same thing, as follows:

```
i  1▾ <script>
   2        var charisma = 11;
   3        var intelligence = 11;
   4        var strength = 10;
   5        var armor = 10;
   6        var can_defeat_dragon = false;
   7
   8        if((charisma > 10 && intelligence > 10)
   9▾          || (armor > 100 && strength > 100)) {
   10              can_defeat_dragon = true;
   11       }
```

Can you defeat a dragon? Yes

Above, we have used brackets to separate the two sets of conditions. Below I have written the **if** statement's condition section on one line and added some extra space to make it easier to understand:

```
if(  (charisma > 10 && intelligence > 10) || (armor > 100 && strength > 100)  ) {
```

JavaScript first evaluates (i.e. checks the value of) the condition on the left of the double pipe: **(charisma > 10 && intelligence > 10)** and since this condition is true, the statement runs. Similar to mathematics, JavaScript first evaluates the stuff inside brackets. If we were to change the positions of the extra brackets, we would get erroneous results:

```
   8        if(charisma > 10 && (intelligence > 10
   9▾          || armor > 100) && strength > 100) {
   10              can_defeat_dragon = true;
   11       }
```

Above, I have changed things so that it is now **intelligence** and **armor** that are in brackets: **(intelligence > 10 || armor > 100)**. The meaning of this new **if** statement is that the player should have a **charisma** higher than 10, and an **intelligence** higher than 10 or **armor** higher than 100, and a **strength** greater than 100, in order to be able to defeat a dragon. Now if we set the **charisma** and **intelligence** extremely high, they do nothing to help the player defeat the dragon if they do not also have high strength. By changing the position of brackets, the meaning of the conditionals completely changes.

```
i  1▾ <script>
   2        var charisma = 100;
   3        var intelligence = 100;
   4        var strength = 100;
   5        var armor = 10;
   6        var can_defeat_dragon = false;
   7
   8        if(charisma > 10 && (intelligence > 10
   9▾          || armor > 100) && strength > 100) {
   10              can_defeat_dragon = true;
   11       }
```

Can you defeat a dragon? No

5. Further Loops

We have already looked at **while** loops, used for making JavaScript repeatedly do something. There are other types of loops that we use in programming, one of which is the **for** loop. But before we talk about **for** loops, we have to talk about incrementing and decrementing.

Incrementing and Decrementing

If you have a variable with a number inside it, such as 5, you can increase its value by 1 (to make it 6) as follows:

```
i  1 ▾ <script>
   2        var my_number = 5;
   3        my_number = my_number + 1;
   4        document.write(my_number);
   5    </script>
```
6

Above, even though we assign the number 5 to **my_number** on line 2, since we add one two it and assign the result back to the variable on line 3, the number 6 gets printed out in the preview area.

JavaScript provides us with a shorthand for doing this, as follows:

```
i  1 ▾ <script>
   2        var my_number = 5;
   3        my_number++;
   4        document.write(my_number);
   5    </script>
```
6

The meaning of the above code is the same as before, but we are now using the *increment operator* (two plus signs without spaces). When we put **++** after a variable name, we tell JavaScript to increase the variable's value by one. Behind the scenes, JavaScript checks the variable's value (which in the above example is the number 5), finds out the result of increasing it by one (which is the number 6), then changes the variable by putting the new number inside it.

We also have the *decrement operator* which is made up of two minus signs. This operator decreases a variable's value by one:

```
i  1 ▾ <script>
   2        var my_number = 5;
   3        my_number--;
   4        document.write(my_number);
   5    </script>
```
4

Above, the number 4 gets printed out because on line 3 we use the decrement operator to decrease the value of **my_number** by one. Note that on line 3 we have a semicolon at the end. This is necessary since **my_number--** is a complete statement and needs to be terminated by a semicolon like any other statement. If we repeatedly decrement a variable, each time we take one away from it. Below, we turn the variable's value from 5 to zero using five decrement statements:

```
i  1 ▾ <script>
   2        var my_number = 5;
   3        my_number--;
   4        my_number--;
   5        my_number--;
   6        my_number--;
   7        my_number--;
   8        document.write(my_number);
   9    </script>
```
0

For loops

Below is an example of a very simple **for** loop:

```
i  1 ▾ <script>
   2 ▾     for(var i = 1; i < 5; i++) {
   3            document.write('Hello!' + '<br>');
   4        }
   5    </script>
   6
```
Hello!
Hello!
Hello!
Hello!

In the above block of code, we tell JavaScript to print out "Hello" four times. To understand what is going on, let's examine the stuff on line 2 in detail. After the for, we have brackets that contain three sections of code, like this:

for(section 1 ; section 2 ; section 3)

Each section is separated from the others by a semicolon. In the first section, we declare a variable we want to use to control how many times the loop will run. This first section is a simple variable declaration like we have already seen numerous times:

var i = 1;

The variable is named **i**. It is common practice to name this variable **i**, but it can be named anything else we want.

In the second section, we declare the condition that JavaScript should check with every iteration of the loop (each time the code of the loop runs). The condition we have provided above is **i < 5**. This means that the loop should run as long as the value of the variable **i** is less than five.

In the third section, we give JavaScript a statement that should run with each iteration of the loop. This section is generally used to make a change to the value of **i** the affects whether the loop continues running or not. The statement we have given it is an increment statement: **i++**. This means that every time the loop runs, the value of **i** should be increased by one.

Let's now take another look at our example **for** loop:

```
i  1 ▾ <script>
   2 ▾     for(var i = 1; i < 5; i++) {        Hello!
   3            document.write('Hello!' + '<br>');   Hello!
   4        }                                    Hello!
   5 </script>                                   Hello!
   6
```

When JavaScript runs the above code, what takes place is that first it creates a variable named **i**. Then it checks whether the variable satisfies the condition **i < 5**. Since it does, JavaScript runs the code inside the **for** loop's curly braces, so that a "Hello!" is printed out followed by a new line. Once JavaScript gets to the bottom of the **for** loop (once it gets to the closing curly brace), it runs the statement in the third section of the code on line 2, increasing the value of **i** by one, so that now **i** will have a value of 2 behind the scenes.

Then JavaScript goes back to the top of the loop, checks the condition on line 2 to see if it is still true (it checks whether two is less than five), then runs the code again, then at the end increases **i** by one, then jumps back to the top, and so on and so forth.

The first section of the code on line 2, where we declare the variable **i**, only runs once at the beginning. The other two sections run with every iteration.

We can make use of the variable **i** inside the loop's code. We can for example check what its value is with each iteration:

```
1  <script>
2      for(var i = 1; i < 5; i++) {
3          document.write(i + '<br>');
4          document.write('Hello!' + '<br>');
5      }
6  </script>
7
8
9
10
11
```

```
1
Hello!
2
Hello!
3
Hello!
4
Hello!
```

Above, we see that at first the value of **i** is 1. It increases with each iteration until it becomes 4. Then the loop ends. The reason the loop ends is that at the end of the fourth iteration, JavaScript runs **i++**, which turns the value of **i** into 5. Then it checks whether **i** is less than five before deciding whether to run the loop another time. Since the value of **i** is no longer less than five, the loop finishes running.

Let's now check out a new example:

```
1  <script>
2      for(var i = 1; i > -5; i--) {
3          document.write(i + '<br>');
4      }
5  </script>
6
7
8
9
```

```
1
0
-1
-2
-3
-4
```

Above, we start out by declaring **i** to be 1. But the condition is now different, **i > -5** means that the loop should run as long as **i** is greater than minus five. In the third section on line 2, we have **i--** (rather than **i++**). This means that we decrease the value of **i** by one with each iteration. The result, as you see, is that the value of **i** decreases each time until it reaches -4, at which point the loop finishes.

Similar to a **while** loop, **for** loops can lead to infinite loops that never finish running and that cause your browser to crash. Below is an example of an infinite **for** loop:

```
i  1▾  <script>
   2▾      for(var i = 1; i > -5; i++) {
   3             document.write(i + '<br>');
   4         }
   5   </script>
```

The problem with this loop is in the third section on line 2 (everything else is similar to the code in the previous screenshot). We are telling JavaScript to print out the value of **i** as long as it is greater than minus five. The problem is that since we are increasing i with each iteration (since it is now **i++** rather than **i--**), *the value of **i** will never stop being greater than -5.* In fact, the value of **i** will continue increasing indefinitely, so that the condition **i > -5** will always be true. The result is that this loop will continue running until your computer uses all the energy in the universe, or until your browser crashes, whichever comes first.

If the syntax of the **for** loop still seems mysterious and difficult to understand, this is perfectly fine. It will take much practice before it starts to make intuitive sense.

Moving on, below we have a for loop that uses neither the increment or decrement operator in the third section on line 2. It rather uses the new statement **i = i * 2**. This means that JavaScript should multiple the value of **i** with every iteration.

```
i  1▾  <script>                                    1
   2▾      for(var i = 1; i < 100; i = i * 2) {
   3             document.write(i + '<br>');         2
   4         }                                       4
   5   </script>
   6                                                 8
   7                                                16
   8                                                32
   9                                                64
  10
```

The result is obvious. JavaScript keeps doubling the value of **i** and printing it out until the condition **i < 100** stops being true.

Anything you put in the third section of a **for** loop should be a *complete JavaScript statement*. If we had merely put **i * 2**, we would have caused an infinite loop:

```
i  1▾  <script>
   2▾      for(var i = 1; i < 100; i * 2) {
   3             document.write(i + '<br>');
   4         }
   5   </script>
```

Above, with each iteration, JavaScript multiplies **i** by two then *throws away the result*, since we do not have **i =** in front of it. We are basically telling JavaScript to run the loop as long as **i** is less than 100 without telling it to do anything to the value of **i**, so that **i** forever remains 1.

To understand this better, consider the following code:

```
i  1▾ <script>
   2       var i = 1;
   3       i * 2;
   4       document.write(i);
   5  </script>
```
1

A beginner might expect the code on line 3 to cause the value of **i** to become 2. But as you can see in the preview, when we print out the value of **i** on line 4, we get 1 rather than 2. The code on line 3 is actually useless, because it should be **i = i * 2**. If we merely write **i * 2**, this tells JavaScript to find out the result of **i** times two, but it does not tell it to do anything with the result, so JavaScript performs the calculation behind the scenes then throws away the result.

Here is an example:

```
i  1▾ <script>
   2       var i = 1;
   3       5 * 5 * 5;
   4       document.write(i);
   5  </script>
```
1

Above, on line 3 we tell JavaScript to multiply five by five by five. But since we do not tell JavaScript to do anything with the result, the calculation takes place behind the scenes then JavaScript throws away the result. In order for JavaScript not to throw away the result, we have to either tell it to print it out, as follows:

```
i  1▾ <script>
   2       var i = 1;
   3       document.write(5 * 5 * 5);
   4       document.write('<br>');
   5       document.write(i);
   6  </script>
```
125
1

Or we have to put the result inside some variable, as follows:

```
i  1▾ <script>
   2       var i = 1;
   3       var j = 5 * 5 * 5;
   4       document.write(i);
   5       document.write('<br>');
   6       document.write(j);
   7  </script>
```
1
125

Below, we have another example of a useless piece of JavaScript:

```
i  1▾ <script>
   2        'hello';
   3    </script>
```

The above is perfectly valid JavaScript code, similar to writing **5 * 5 * 5**. It tells JavaScript to evaluate the value of **'hello'** but without telling it to do anything with it. So JavaScript dutifully looks at the string **'hello'** and sees that it is good, then forgets about it. The code works, it just doesn't do anything we humans would consider useful.

Never loops

A never loop is a loop that never runs. Below is an example:

```
i  1▾ <script>
   2▾      for(var i = 1; i > 50; i++) {
   3            document.write(i + '<br>');
   4        }
   5    </script>
```

On line 3, we tell JavaScript to continue running the loop as long as **i** is greater than 50. But since **i** is 1 at the beginning, the condition is false from the start, so the loop ends immediately without printing anything out.

```
i  1▾ <script>
   2        var my_number = 0;
   3▾      while(my_number === 1) {
   4            document.write(my_number);
   5        }
   6    </script>
```

Above, on line 3, we are saying the loop should run as long as **my_number** equals 1. But since on line 2 we have declared that **my_number** is zero, this condition is false from the start, so the code inside the while loop's curly braces never runs. JavaScript simply ignores it and goes on to run any code that might be below it, as follows:

```
i  1▾ <script>
   2        var my_number = 0;
   3▾      while(my_number === 1) {
   4            document.write(my_number);
   5        }
   6        document.write('Here we are.');
   7    </script>
```

Here we are.

6. Functions

In programming, functions allow us to name a block of code and reuse it later on. Below is an example:

```
 i  1 ▾ <script>
    2 ▾     function newline() {
    3             document.write('<br>');
    4         }
    5
    6         document.write('First line.');
    7         newline();
    8         document.write('Second line.');
    9   </script>
```

First line.
Second line.

On lines 2-4, we define a function named **newline()**. The function name is followed by brackets for reasons that will become clear later on. After the brackets we have curly braces, then the actual code of the function. What this function does is that it prints out a new line. You see the function used on line 7. On line 6, we write out a line. On line 7 we *call* the **newline** function, and on line 8 we write out a second line.

A function name can be anything we want, similar to variable names, and similar to variable names, there are some characters you are not allowed to use in the name, such as dashes.

When we write **newline();** on line 7, it is as if we had written **document.write('<br>');**. Behind the scenes, every time JavaScript sees the statement **newline()**, it performs the action inside the **newline** function.

Below, we call the **newline()** function twice, causing two new lines to be printed out:

```
i   1 ▾ <script>
    2 ▾     function newline() {
    3             document.write('<br>');
    4         }
    5
    6         document.write('First line.');
    7         newline();
    8         newline();
    9         document.write('Second line.');
   10   </script>
```

First line.

Second line.

When we define the **newline()** function on lines 2-4, this does not cause anything to happen just yet. JavaScript stores the code inside the function until we *call* it. Above, we call the function twice, on lines 7 and 8.

If we remove the calls to **newline()**, the function will not do anything:

```
i   1 ▾ <script>
    2 ▾     function newline() {
    3             document.write('<br>');
    4         }
    5
    6         document.write('First line.');
    7         document.write('Second line.');
    8   </script>
```

First line.Second line.

When you declare a function, you are telling JavaScript to hold this piece of code in memory until you have a need for it later on.

Below we have a little program that greets a user based on their language. If the user's language is English, the program says "Hello", while if the user's language is French, it says "Bonjour":

```
i   1 ▾ <script>
    2         var user_name = 'James';
    3         var user_language = 'English';
    4
    5 ▾     function greetings() {
    6 ▾         if(user_language === 'English') {
    7                 document.write('Hello');
    8             }
    9 ▾         else if(user_language === 'French') {
   10                 document.write('Bonjour');
   11             }
   12         }
   13
   14         greetings();
   15         document.write(' ');
   16         document.write(user_name);
   17         document.write('!');
   18   </script>
```

Hello James!

Inside the **greetings()** function on lines 5 to 12, we check the **user_language** variable, and based on its value, we either write out "Hello" or "Bonjour". Above, you see the **else if** statement, which is used to check a condition once the condition before it proves to be false. We are telling JavaScript: If the language is English, then do this, *but if* the language is French, then do this other thing. We could have also added an else at the end to tell JavaScript what to do if the language is neither English nor French.

On lines 14-17, we start to actually write out some stuff. First, we call the **greetings()** function, which ends up writing out a "Hello". Then we write out a space (line 15), the user's name (line 16) and finally an exclamation mark (line 17).

Every time we call the greetings() function, JavaScript checks the user's language to see whether it should write out a "Hello" or a "Bonjour".

Below, we have the same code as above while adding some additional lines to it starting from line 20. We change the **user_name** variable to "Marcel" and we change the **user_language** to "French".

```
 1 ▾ <script>
 2        var user_name = 'James';
 3        var user_language = 'English';
 4
 5 ▾      function greetings() {
 6 ▾          if(user_language === 'English') {
 7                  document.write('Hello');
 8          }
 9 ▾          else if(user_language === 'French') {
10                  document.write('Bonjour');
11          }
12      }
13
14      greetings();
15      document.write(' ');
16      document.write(user_name);
17      document.write('!');
18      document.write('<br>');
19
20      user_name = 'Marcel';
21      user_language = 'French';
22      greetings();
23      document.write(' ');
24      document.write(user_name);
25      document.write('!');
26      document.write('<br>');
27 </script>
```

Hello James!
Bonjour Marcel!

Above, on line 22 we have another call to the **greetings()** function, but note that this time it writes out a "Bonjour", because we changed the user's language on line 21 to French.

Below, I have renamed the greetings() function to **greet_user()** and added some extra code to its end:

```
5 ▾     function greet_user() {
6 ▾         if(user_language === 'English') {
7              document.write('Hello');
8          }
9 ▾         else if(user_language === 'French') {
10             document.write('Bonjour');
11         }
12         document.write(' ');
13         document.write(user_name);
14         document.write('!');
15     }
```

Now, the function checks the user's language and greets them, and *also* prints out a space, the user's name and an exclamation mark. All of these actions happen every time we call **greet_user()**, as follows:

```
i  1 ▾ <script>
   2       var user_name = 'James';
   3       var user_language = 'English';
   4
   5 ▾     function greet_user() {
   6 ▾         if(user_language === 'English') {
   7              document.write('Hello');
   8          }
   9 ▾         else if(user_language === 'French') {
   10             document.write('Bonjour');
   11         }
   12         document.write(' ');
   13         document.write(user_name);
   14         document.write('!');
   15     }
   16
   17     greet_user();
   18     document.write('<br>');
   19
   20     user_name = 'Marcel';
   21     user_language = 'French';
   22     greet_user();
   23     document.write('<br>');
   24 </script>
```

Hello James!
Bonjour Marcel!

Above, on line 17 we call **greet_user()**, which prints out "Hello James!". Then we print out a new line on line 18. Next we change the user's name to "Marcel" and the user's language to "French", then call **greet_user()** again on line 22. This time it prints out "Bonjour Marcel!".

The great power of functions is that they help us use the same piece of code in multiple places, which helps make our programs shorter and easier to understand.

Moving on, below we have a different program that calculates an employee's new salary based on their performance rating. The rating can either be A, B, or C.

```
1  <script>
2      var employee_performance = 'A';
3      var salary = 50000;
4
5      function show_new_salary() {
6          document.write('Your new salary is ');
7          if(employee_performance === 'A') {
8              document.write(salary * 1.1);
9          }
10         else if(employee_performance === 'B') {
11             document.write(salary * 1.05);
12         }
13         else {
14             document.write(salary);
15         }
16     }
17
18     show_new_salary();
19 </script>
```

Your new salary is 55000.00000000001

The **show_new_salary()** function writes out "Your new salary is " followed by a number. If the **employee_performance** variable equals "A", the salary is multiplied by 1.1, meaning it is increased by 10%. If the performance is "B", it is instead multiplied by 1.05, meaning it is increased by only 5%. And if their performance is something else, no promotion is applied.

Since on line 2 we declared the performance as "A", when we call **show_new_salary()** on line 18, the promotion on line 8 is applied and printed out, which is what you see in the preview area. The salary shown is 55000, a 10% increase over 50000.

You may notice that the salary shown is not exactly 55000, it is rather 55000.00000000001. That is caused by the way JavaScript performs calculations behind the scenes. JavaScript performs *approximate* calculations when doing things like multiplication and division, which result in strange results like the above. The root cause has to do with the way numbers are represented inside the computer's memory. To avoid that, we have to use can use certain mathematical operations to round the resulting number to an integer:

```
i  1 ▾  <script>
   2        var employee_performance = 'A';
   3        var salary = 50000;
   4
   5 ▾      function show_new_salary() {
   6            document.write('Your new salary is ');
   7            var new_salary = salary;
   8
   9 ▾          if(employee_performance === 'A') {
  10                new_salary = Math.floor(salary * 1.1);
  11            }
  12 ▾          else if(employee_performance === 'B') {
  13                new_salary = Math.floor(salary * 1.05);
  14            }
  15 ▾          else {
  16
  17            }
  18            document.write(new_salary);
  19        }
  20
  21        show_new_salary();
  22  </script>
```

Your new salary is 55000

Above, I have made some changes to the **show_new_salary()** function. On line 7, I declare a new variable called **new_salary** and place inside it the number that is already inside **salary**. This means that we assume the new salary is the same as the old salary unless proven otherwise later on. Since the **employee_performance** is "A", the code on line 10 runs. In this line of code, perform the same calculation as before by multiplying the **salary** by 1.1 to increase it by 10%. But this time we have enclosed the calculation between the **Math.floor()** function. The **Math.floor()** function is a built-in JavaScript function that rounds down a number with decimal points to an integer. It takes a number and shows us what the number is if we take away everything after the decimal point.

Finally, on line 18 we print out **new_salary**, which is 55000.

Notice that on line 16, the **else** statement is now empty. That is because there is nothing for the **else** statement to do anymore. Since on line 7 we assume that **new_salary** is the same as **salary**, if the performance is anything besides "A" or "B", the **new_salary** will be the same as **salary** without any need for additional statements. Since the **else** statement is empty, we can remove it:

```
 9 ▾      if(employee_performance === 'A') {
10            new_salary = Math.floor(salary * 1.1);
11        }
12 ▾      else if(employee_performance === 'B') {
13            new_salary = Math.floor(salary * 1.05);
14        }
15        document.write(new_salary);
16    }
```

To illustrate that it is still functioning correctly, I will now change the performance to "C":

```
 1 ▾ <script>
 2       var employee_performance = 'C';
 3       var salary = 50000;
 4
 5 ▾     function show_new_salary() {
 6           document.write('Your new salary is ');
 7           var new_salary = salary;
 8
 9 ▾         if(employee_performance === 'A') {
10               new_salary = Math.floor(salary * 1.1);
11           }
12 ▾         else if(employee_performance === 'B') {
13               new_salary = Math.floor(salary * 1.05);
14           }
15           document.write(new_salary);
16       }
17
18       show_new_salary();
19 </script>
```

Your new salary is 50000

As you can see, the salary remains at 50000, because inside the **show_new_salary()** function JavaScript sets **new_salary** to **salary** on line 7, then checks whether the performance is "A" or "B", and since it is not, it ends up writing out **new_salary** without making changes to it.

Below, after printing out the first employee's new salary, we change the variables, presumably dealing with a different employee whose old salary is 75000 and whose performance is "A":

```
18       show_new_salary();
19       document.write('<br>');
20
21       employee_performance = 'A';
22       salary = 75000;
23       show_new_salary();
24 </script>
```

Here is the result:

Your new salary is 50000
Your new salary is 82500

COMPUTER PROGRAMMING FOR COMPLETE BEGINNERS

Functions with inputs

In everyday programming, most functions take *inputs*, something our functions have not done so far. **Math.floor()** is an example of a function that takes inputs: you give it a number, it gives you a result.

Below, we have a function that doubles any number we give to it:

```
i  1 ▾ <script>
   2 ▾     function double_this(number) {
   3           var new_number = number * 2;
   4           return new_number;
   5       }
   6
   7       document.write(double_this(50));
   8 </script>
```

100

On line 2, we declare a function named **double_this()**. This function takes a variable called **number**. And it *returns* a variable named **new_number**. On line 7, we write out the result of **double_this(50)**, which results in 100 being shown in the preview area.

Let's now look at the function definition. A *function definition* is the term we use for the whole block of code in which we define a function, meaning lines 2-5 above. On line 2, inside the brackets we have the word **number**. This causes a variable to be created inside the function with the name of **number**. JavaScript automatically puts inside this variable anything we *pass* to the function when we make use of the function. Since on line 7 we pass the number 50 to the **double_this()** function, this causes the **number** variable to have 50 inside it.

On line 3, we declare a new variable named **new_number**, which has value of **number** multiplied by two. On line 4 we have something new, the **return** statement. In this statement we tell JavaScript what the function should *return*, meaning what the function should "print out" when we use it. Writing **return new_number;** means "whenever this function is called, give back **new_number** as the result".

This can be a bit difficult for a beginner to understand. This is perfectly fine, since here we are dealing with a very complex part of programming. Once you have understood how functions work, you will have mastered the basics of programming.

To further clarify, below I have kept the function the same as before while changing the stuff after it. The meaning of the code is the same as before:

```
i   1▾ <script>
    2▾     function double_this(number) {
    3          var new_number = number * 2;         100
    4          return new_number;
    5      }
    6
    7      var my_number = 50;
    8      var my_doubled_number = double_this(my_number);
    9      document.write(my_doubled_number);
   10  </script>
```

On line 8, I declare the variable **my_doubled_number**. The value we assign to this variable is the result of double_this(my_number). This tells JavaScript to put **my_number** inside the **double_this()** function, then put inside **my_doubled_number** whatever is returned by the function. Think of the function as a machine. Something goes in, something else comes out.

Below we use **double_this()** to double a bunch of different numbers on lines 7, 9 and 11:

```
i   1▾ <script>
    2▾     function double_this(number) {        20
    3          var new_number = number * 2;      40
    4          return new_number;                66
    5      }
    6
    7      document.write(double_this(10));
    8      document.write('<br>');
    9      document.write(double_this(20));
   10      document.write('<br>');
   11      document.write(double_this(33));
   12  </script>
```

Doubling a number is not a very impressive mathematical operation. Let's create a function that checks whether a number is odd or not:

```
i   1▾ <script>
    2▾     function is_odd(number) {
    3          var divided_by_two = number / 2;
    4          var rounded = Math.floor(divided_by_two);
    5▾         if(rounded === divided_by_two) {
    6              return false;
    7          }
    8▾         else {
    9              return true;
   10          }
   11      }
```

What we have inside the above function is an *algorithm*, a word named after the Persian mathematician al-Khwarizmi (died 850 CE). An algorithm is a step-by-step set of instructions for discovering the value of something. On line 2 of the function, we divide the

number variable (the number the user is trying to find out whether it is odd or even) by two. If it is an even number, the division will not lead to a decimal point (for example dividing 20 by two results in 10 without any decimals). While if it is an odd number, the result will contain stuff after the decimal point (for example, dividing 3 by 2 results in 1.5). We use this fact to detect whether a number is odd or even. On line 4, we round down the divided number to the nearest integer. If **divided_by_two** contains a whole number, rounding will have no effect on it (if we divided 20 by 2, the result would be 10, and rounding it would still give us 10). But if it contains a number with stuff after the decimals, rounding it would cause that stuff to be thrown away, so that the **rounded** number ends up being different from **divided_by_two**.

On line 5, we check whether rounding made a difference or not. If **rounded** is exactly the same as **divided_by_two**, it means rounding made no difference, which means **divided_by_two** had no fractional part, which means number is even, therefore we return the boolean value of "false", meaning **number** is not odd. In the **else** part, we return "true", meaning **number** is odd. Below is an example of how we can make use of the **is_odd()** function:

```
1 ▾ <script>
2 ▾     function is_odd(number) {
3           var divided_by_two = number / 2;
4           var rounded = Math.floor(divided_by_two);
5 ▾         if(rounded === divided_by_two) {
6               return false;
7           }
8 ▾         else {
9               return true;
10          }
11      }
12
13      var age = 55;
14      document.write('Your age is ');
15 ▾    if(is_odd(age) === true) {
16          document.write('odd');
17      }
18 ▾    else {
19          document.write('even');
20      }
21  </script>
```

Your age is odd

On line 15, **is_odd(age) === true** means "does the **is_odd()** function return **true** when you pass it the value of the **age** variable? JavaScript runs the **is_odd()** function by putting the number 55 into the **number** variable and performing the rest of the calculations. If on line 9 the value that is returned is **true**, then the code on line 16 runs. Otherwise the code on line 19 runs. Below we change **age** to 22:

```
i  1 ▾ <script>
   2 ▾     function is_odd(number) {
   3           var divided_by_two = number / 2;
   4           var rounded = Math.floor(divided_by_two);
   5 ▾         if(rounded === divided_by_two) {
   6               return false;
   7           }
   8 ▾         else {
   9               return true;
  10           }
  11       }
  12
  13       var age = 22;
  14       document.write('Your age is ');
  15 ▾     if(is_odd(age) === true) {
  16           document.write('odd');
  17       }
  18 ▾     else {
  19           document.write('even');
  20       }
  21   </script>
```

Your age is even

Below, we have a loop in which we use the **is_odd()** function to check whether the numbers from 1 to 9 are odd or even:

```
i  1 ▾ <script>
   2 ▾     function is_odd(number) {
   3           var divided_by_two = number / 2;
   4           var rounded = Math.floor(divided_by_two);
   5 ▾         if(rounded === divided_by_two) {
   6               return false;
   7           }
   8 ▾         else {
   9               return true;
  10           }
  11       }
  12
  13 ▾     for(var i = 1; i < 10; i++) {
  14           document.write('The number ' + i + ' is ');
  15 ▾         if(is_odd(i) === true) {
  16               document.write('odd');
  17           }
  18 ▾         else {
  19               document.write('even');
  20           }
  21           document.write('<br>');
  22       }
  23   </script>
```

The number 1 is odd
The number 2 is even
The number 3 is odd
The number 4 is even
The number 5 is odd
The number 6 is even
The number 7 is odd
The number 8 is even
The number 9 is odd

With each iteration of the loop, JavaScript passes the value of **i** to the **is_odd()** function on line 15, which determines whether the word "odd" will be printed out on line 16 or the word "even" on line 19. Before the end of each iteration, we print out a new line on line 21 so that the next line of text should start on a new line.

Below, we have the same loop as the above converted to a while loop:

```
i   1 ▾ <script>
    2 ▾     function is_odd(number) {
    3           var divided_by_two = number / 2;
    4           var rounded = Math.floor(divided_by_two);
    5 ▾         if(rounded === divided_by_two) {
    6               return false;
    7           }
    8 ▾         else {
    9               return true;
   10           }
   11       }
   12
   13       var number_to_check = 1;
   14 ▾     while(number_to_check < 10) {
   15           document.write('The number ' +
   16             number_to_check + ' is ');
   17 ▾         if(is_odd(number_to_check) === true) {
   18               document.write('odd');
   19           }
   20 ▾         else {
   21               document.write('even');
   22           }
   23           document.write('<br>');
   24
   25           number_to_check++;
   26       }
   27 </script>
```

The number 1 is odd
The number 2 is even
The number 3 is odd
The number 4 is even
The number 5 is odd
The number 6 is even
The number 7 is odd
The number 8 is even
The number 9 is odd

The code should be self-explanatory, except for line 25. Without line 25, the above loop would be an infinite loop, because **number_to_check** will always remain at 1 unless we do something to it inside the loop. If we do nothing to it, the condition on line 14 will always be true. What we do on line 25 is increase the number by one, so that on the next iteration the loop should deal with the number that comes after it. In this way the number eventually reaches 10, which causes the loop to stop running.

Moving on, we can make use of one function to build another function. For example, let's say we want to make an **is_even()** function to check whether a number is even or odd. Instead of building a whole new function from scratch, we can make use of **is_odd()** from before:

```
i   1▾  <script>
    2▾      function is_odd(number) {
    3           var divided_by_two = number / 2;
    4           var rounded = Math.floor(divided_by_two);
    5▾          if(rounded === divided_by_two) {
    6               return false;
    7           }
    8▾          else {
    9               return true;
   10           }
   11       }
   12
   13▾      function is_even(number) {
   14▾          if(is_odd(number) === false) {
   15               return true;
   16           }
   17▾          else {
   18               return false;
   19           }
   20       }
   21  </script>
```

Above, we have the same code as before from lines 2-11. We then have the new **is_even()** function. This function merely checks whether a number is odd using the **is_odd()** function from before. If it is not odd, it returns **true**, otherwise it returns **false**. In this way, the **is_even()** function does not need to do any mathematical heavy lifting, it leaves it all to the **is_odd()** function.

Moving on, earlier we had the following example for calculating an employee's new salary based on their performance:

```
i   1▾  <script>
    2       var employee_performance = 'C';
    3       var salary = 50000;
    4
    5▾      function show_new_salary() {
    6           document.write('Your new salary is ');
    7           var new_salary = salary;
    8
    9▾          if(employee_performance === 'A') {
   10               new_salary = Math.floor(salary * 1.1);
   11           }
   12▾          else if(employee_performance === 'B') {
   13               new_salary = Math.floor(salary * 1.05);
   14           }
   15           document.write(new_salary);
   16       }
   17
   18       show_new_salary();
   19  </script>
```

Your new salary is 50000

The **show_new_salary()** function is not actually a good function in programming because it is making use of variables outside of it. If you move this function to a different web page, the function might fail miserably if someone forgets to declare the

employee_performance and **salary** variables above it. In real-world programming, the code might go on for thousands of lines and you can never rely on some variable being available. To turn it into a good function, we have to turn it into a function that take the employee performance and salary as inputs, rather than accessing them randomly. Below is the improved example:

```
i  1 ▾ <script>
   2       var employee_performance = 'A';
   3       var salary = 45000;
   4
   5 ▾     function show_new_salary(salary, perf) {
   6           document.write('Your new salary is ');
   7           var new_salary = salary;
   8
   9 ▾         if(perf === 'A') {
  10               new_salary = Math.floor(salary * 1.1);
  11           }
  12 ▾         else if(perf === 'B') {
  13               new_salary = Math.floor(salary * 1.05);
  14           }
  15           document.write(new_salary);
  16       }
  17
  18       show_new_salary(salary, employee_performance);
  19 </script>
```

Your new salary is 49500

Above, we have changed the **show_new_salary()** function so that it now takes two inputs, as declared on line 5. The two inputs are separated by a comma. The first input is **salary**, the second is **perf**, short for performance. Everything else functions like before. On line 18, when using **show_new_salary()**, we now have to pass it the variables **salary** and **employee_performance**. The **show_new_salary()** function is now independent of the code that is outside of it. For example, we can rename the **employee_performance** variable on line 2 to **performance**, we also change the code on line 18 to say performance rather than **employee_performance**. Now the code continues working like before even though we made no changes at all to the show_new_salary() function:

```
i   1 ▾ <script>
    2       var performance = 'A';
    3       var salary = 45000;
    4
    5 ▾     function show_new_salary(salary, perf) {
    6           document.write('Your new salary is ');
    7           var new_salary = salary;
    8
    9 ▾         if(perf === 'A') {
   10               new_salary = Math.floor(salary * 1.1);
   11           }
   12 ▾         else if(perf === 'B') {
   13               new_salary = Math.floor(salary * 1.05);
   14           }
   15           document.write(new_salary);
   16       }
   17
   18       show_new_salary(salary, performance);
   19 </script>
```

Your new salary is 49500

In the earlier, not-so-good example where the **show_new_salary()** function wasn't taking inputs, if we had changed the names of the variables on lines 2 or 3, we would have also had to change the **show_new_salary()** function. But now that the function operates according to inputs, it does not care about the variable names outside of it. It operates in a separate universe of its own; it has become a machine that takes something and spits something out.

As it should be clear by now, the variable names inside the function are unrelated to those outside. Below we rename **salary** to **pay** inside the function:

```
i   1 ▾ <script>
    2       var performance = 'A';
    3       var salary = 45000;
    4
    5 ▾     function show_new_salary(pay, perf) {
    6           document.write('Your new salary is ');
    7           var new_pay = pay;
    8
    9 ▾         if(perf === 'A') {
   10               new_pay = Math.floor(pay * 1.1);
   11           }
   12 ▾         else if(perf === 'B') {
   13               new_pay = Math.floor(pay * 1.05);
   14           }
   15           document.write(new_pay);
   16       }
   17
   18       show_new_salary(salary, performance);
   19 </script>
```

Your new salary is 49500

Above, everything continues functioning normally because the function does not care about the variable names outside. It only cares about what is passed to it by JavaScript. Whatever we pass to it on line 18 ends up inside the function's **pay** and **perf** variables.

To clarify further, we have a simpler, although more absurd, example:

```
i  1▾ <script>
   2      var number = 5;
   3▾     function double_monkey(monkey) {
   4          return monkey * 2;
   5      }
   6      document.write(double_monkey(number));
   7  </script>
```
10

Above, we have a **double_monkey()** function that doubles anything number passed to it. When making use of the function on line 6, we have to pass it the **number** variable. But inside the function, the function is free to call this variable anything it wants. In this case, it calls it **monkey**. To make it even simpler, below I remove the **number** variable:

```
i  1▾ <script>
   2▾     function double_monkey(monkey) {
   3          return monkey * 2;
   4      }
   5      document.write(double_monkey(5));
   6  </script>
```
10

Above, we pass the number 5 to the **double_monkey()** function on line 5, which turns it into 10.

At this point, we have covered the basics of functions. If you are still a bit unclear on how functions exactly work, continue reading and it should become clearer as you see more examples of functions in action.

7. String Manipulation

Performing operations on strings is part of daily life for a programmer, for this reason programming languages offer a vast array of functionality to help us work with strings. In the following example, we print out the first letter of the word "cat":

```
1 ▼ <script>
2       var word = 'cat';
3       var first_letter = word[0];
4       document.write(first_letter);
5   </script>
```

c

On line 3, we use a special syntax that lets us access any character of a string by providing its place in the string. The meaning of **word[0]** is "the character in the **word** variable that is at position zero". In programming, we often start counting up from zero, rather than one, so position zero means the first character. Below, we change **word[0]** to **word[1]**, which ends up printing the second character for the **word** variable (the letter "a" in "cat"):

```
1 ▼ <script>
2       var word = 'cat';
3       var second_letter = word[1];
4       document.write(second_letter);
5   </script>
```

a

Below we have an even simpler example:

```
1 ▼ <script>
2       document.write('Hello there!'[11]);
3   </script>
```

!

When we write **'Hello there!'[11]**, it means "get the character that is at position 11 of this string", which happens to be the exclamation mark.

Changing case

Below, we use JavaScript's built-in **toUpperCase()** function to capitalize a word:

```
1 ▾ <script>
2        var animal = 'dog';
3        var capital_animal = 'dog'.toUpperCase();
4
5        document.write(animal + ' ' + capital_animal);
6 </script>
```

dog DOG

The syntax **'dog'.toUpperCase()** is unusual because nothing is passed to the **toUpperCase()** function like you would expect. What we have here is a special syntax that we use when calling one of JavaScript's build-in functions on a particular type of data (a string, a number, or something else). The **toUpperCase()** function can only be used with strings, if you use it with a number you get an error:

```
1 ▾ <script>
2        var number = 5;
3        var number_capitalized = number.toUpperCase();
4        document.write(number_capitalized);
5 </script>
```

When we run the above nonsensical code, we get no output. If we look at the console, this is what we see:

```
⊗ ▶Uncaught TypeError: number.toUpperCase is not a function
       at <anonymous>:3:37
```

JavaScript says **toUpperCase()** is not a function because in the world of numbers, this function does not exist. It only exists in the world of strings.

When calling a function like **toUpperCase()**, it does not matter whether you call it on a variable that contains a string or on a string directly:

```
1 ▾ <script>
2        var my_string = 'This is a line of text.';
3        var my_string_capitalized = my_string.toUpperCase();
4        document.write(my_string_capitalized);
5 </script>
```

THIS IS A LINE OF TEXT.

The above has the same result as this:

```
1 ▾ <script>
2        var my_string_capitalized = 'This is a line of text.'.toUpperCase();
3        document.write(my_string_capitalized);
4 </script>
```

THIS IS A LINE OF TEXT.

The counterpart to **toUpperCase()** is **toLowerCase()**. Below we have the same code from above, but we print out a new line of text which is made up of the previous line turned to lowercase:

```
i  1▾ <script>
   2       var my_string_capitalized = 'This is a line of text.'.toUpperCase();
   3       document.write(my_string_capitalized);
   4       var my_string_uncapitalized = my_string_capitalized.toLowerCase();
   5       document.write('<br>');
   6       document.write(my_string_uncapitalized);
   7  </script>
```

THIS IS A LINE OF TEXT.
this is a line of text.

Moving on, below we have a function that capitalizes the first letter of any word passed to it. The example brings together much of what we have learned so far and it will require some time to explain, therefore do not worry if at first it looks a bit overwhelming:

```
i  1▾ <script>
   2▾      function capitalizeFirstLetter(word) {
   3            var first_letter = word[0];
   4            first_letter = first_letter.toUpperCase();
   5            var result = first_letter;
   6▾           for(var i = 1; i < word.length; i++) {
   7                result = result + word[i];
   8            }
   9            return result;
   10       }
   11
   12       var word = 'cat';
   13       var first_letter_capitalized
   14           = capitalizeFirstLetter(word);
   15       document.write(first_letter_capitalized);
   16  </script>
```

Cat

Try to read the code and guess how it works before reading my explanation. You should try to do this with every example; the more code you read, the better you will get at understanding how it works.

Inside the **capitalizeFirstLetter()** function, on line 3 we get the first letter of the **word** variable and put it inside the **first_letter** variable. We can check that this is functioning correctly by writing the variable's contents out (line 4 below):

```
i  1▾ <script>
   2▾      function capitalizeFirstLetter(word) {
   3            var first_letter = word[0];
   4            document.write(first_letter + '<br>');
```

c
Cat

As you see in the preview area, a letter "c" is printed followed by a new line. The letter "c" is still lowercase since the uppercasing is done on the next line. Below I have moved the **document.write()** to line 5, after the **first_letter** is made uppercase. As you see in the preview area, now an uppercase "C" is printed out:

```
 i  1 ▾ <script>
    2 ▾     function capitalizeFirstLetter(word) {
    3            var first_letter = word[0];
    4            first_letter = first_letter.toUpperCase();
    5            document.write(first_letter + '<br>');
```
C
Cat

Let's now take another look at the function without any of the additional document.write() statements we added above:

```
    2 ▾     function capitalizeFirstLetter(word) {
    3            var first_letter = word[0];
    4            first_letter = first_letter.toUpperCase();
    5            var result = first_letter;
    6 ▾         for(var i = 1; i < word.length; i++) {
    7                result = result + word[i];
    8            }
    9            return result;
   10        }
```

On line 5, we declare a new variable named **result**. This variable will be a container for the uppercased word. At first we place the first letter inside it, later on we add the rest of the letters. Next we have a for loop. In this loop, we go over the contents of the **word** variable letter by letter, each time adding the letter to the end of the **result** variable.

Since on line 6 we declare the variable i to be 1, when on line 7 JavaScript reads **result + word[i]** the first time, it sees it as **result + word[1]**. On the next iteration, JavaScript increases **i** to 2, so that this time **word[i]** means **word[2]**. With each iteration the next letter of the **word** variable is added to the end of **result**, until the loop is done.

The loops condition on line 6 is **i < word.length**. This means that the loop should run as long as **i** is less than the length of the word variable.

Below I have added two new **document.write()** statements in order to clarify what is happening inside the loop when JavaScript executes it:

```
 i  1 ▾ <script>
    2 ▾     function capitalizeFirstLetter(word) {
    3            var first_letter = word[0];
    4            first_letter = first_letter.toUpperCase();
    5            var result = first_letter;
    6 ▾         for(var i = 1; i < word.length; i++) {
    7                result = result + word[i];
    8                document.write('The value of i is: ' + i + '<br>');
    9                document.write('The value of result is: ' + result + '<br>');
   10            }
   11            return result;
   12        }
```
The value of i is: 1
The value of result is: Ca
The value of i is: 2
The value of result is: Cat
Cat

As you would expect, at first, meaning during the first iteration of the loop, the value of **i** is 1, since we declared it to be 1 on line 6 when we wrote **var i = 1**. During the first iteration the value of **result** is "Ca". That is because before the loop, on line 5, we put "C" inside it. Then inside the loop, on line 7, we put "a" inside it, so that it becomes "Ca". Once JavaScript reaches the bottom of the loop, it increase **i** by one, then it starts from the top again. As you can see in the preview, the loop only runs twice, since the word "cat" has three letters and the loop is designed to only work on the parts of the word that are supposed to be lowercase, so it only deals with the "at" part. At the end of the second iteration, JavaScript increases **i** by one so that it becomes 3. Once it is three, it no longer satisfies the loop's condition of **i < word.length**, since **i** is now 3 and **word.length** is also 3.

Once the loop stops running, we have a return statement on line 11 that returns the **result** variable. Below, I have changed the word "cat" to "dinosaur" on line 14:

```
1  <script>
2      function capitalizeFirstLetter(word) {
3          var first_letter = word[0];
4          first_letter = first_letter.toUpperCase();
5          var result = first_letter;
6          for(var i = 1; i < word.length; i++) {
7              result = result + word[i];
8              document.write('The value of i is: ' + i + '<br>');
9              document.write('The value of result is: ' + result + '<br>');
10         }
11         return result;
12     }
13
14     var word = 'dinosaur';
15     var first_letter_capitalized
16         = capitalizeFirstLetter(word);
17     document.write(first_letter_capitalized);
18  </script>
19
20
```

The value of i is: 1
The value of result is: Di
The value of i is: 2
The value of result is: Din
The value of i is: 3
The value of result is: Dino
The value of i is: 4
The value of result is: Dinos
The value of i is: 5
The value of result is: Dinosa
The value of i is: 6
The value of result is: Dinosau
The value of i is: 7
The value of result is: Dinosaur
Dinosaur

As you see in the preview area, the loop now runs many more times, since the word "dinosaur" is much longer than "cat'. Thanks to the fact that in the for loop we tell JavaScript to run the loop as long as **i** is less than **word.length**, no matter what word we pass to the function, the loop always runs exactly the number of times needed.

Using a loop is actually the hard way of doing things. We could accomplish the same thing using JavaScript's **substring()** function, which allows us to extract part of a string.

```
i  1▾ <script>
   2▾    function capitalizeFirstLetter(word) {
   3          var first_letter = word[0];
   4          first_letter = first_letter.toUpperCase();
   5          var rest_of_the_word = word.substring(1, word.length);
   6          var result = first_letter + rest_of_the_word;
   7          return result;
   8      }
   9
  10      var word = 'dinosaur';
  11      var first_letter_capitalized
  12          = capitalizeFirstLetter(word);
  13      document.write(first_letter_capitalized);
  14  </script>
```

Dinosaur

Above, I have replaced the loop with lines 5 and 6. On line 5, we use the **substring()** function to get the rest of the word after getting its first letter. The **substring()** function takes two numbers corresponding to the range of the characters we wish to extract. Below is a simple example of using the **substring()** function to get the first two letters of the word "cat":

```
i  1▾ <script>
   2      document.write('cat'.substring(0, 2));
   3  </script>
```

ca

Writing **substring(0, 2)** tells JavaScript to put together **'cat'[0]** and **'cat'[1]** and show us the result. It has the same meaning as this:

```
i  1▾ <script>
   2      document.write('cat'[0] + 'cat'[1]);
   3  </script>
```

ca

The second number we give to **substring()** tells JavaScript where it should stop. This number is not inclusive; **substring(0,2)** means "get us the characters at position 0 and 1 but stop before position 2". This can be confusing for programmers, so there is no shame in having to look up this function again and again for months until you get used to it.

Back to our example:

```
i  1▾ <script>
   2▾    function capitalizeFirstLetter(word) {
   3          var first_letter = word[0];
   4          first_letter = first_letter.toUpperCase();
   5          var rest_of_the_word = word.substring(1, word.length);
   6          var result = first_letter + rest_of_the_word;
   7          return result;
   8      }
   9
  10      var word = 'dinosaur';
  11      var first_letter_capitalized
  12          = capitalizeFirstLetter(word);
  13      document.write(first_letter_capitalized);
  14  </script>
```

Dinosaur

Above, on line 5 we give the **substring()** function **word.length** as its second argument (we call the stuff we pass to a function its "arguments", so **substring()** has two arguments, while **capitalizeFirstLetter()** has only one argument). Since the length of "dinosaur" is 8, JavaScript sees this as **substring(1, 8)**, which means that **substring()** should get the letters starting from the second position and stopping before the 8th position. Below is an illustration of how this works:

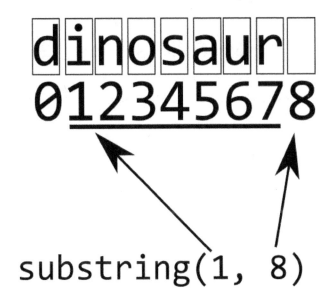

Since JavaScript starts counting the positions from zero rather than one, position 1 is actually the second letter of the word. We tell JavaScript to stop at position 8, which as you see above is empty. So JavaScript ends up getting everything from position 1 to position 7, or "inosaur". The way the **substring()** function works is unintuitive and even experienced programmers will have to occasionally look it up to remember how it works.

On line 6 of our code, we concatenate **first_letter** with **rest_of_the_word**, and place the result inside **result**. On the next line we return the **result** variable.

An experienced programmer can shorten the **capitalizeFirstLetter()** to a single line, as follows:

```
 1 ▾ <script>
 2 ▾     function capitalizeFirstLetter(word) {
 3             return word[0].toUpperCase() + word.substring(1, word.length);
 4         }
 5
 6         var word = 'dinosaur';
 7         var first_letter_capitalized
 8             = capitalizeFirstLetter(word);
 9         document.write(first_letter_capitalized);
10     </script>
```

Dinosaur

Beginners to programming often feel tempted to write code like the above because it looks clever. It accomplishes so much in so little space. But clever code is not always good code, since readability matters. Writing a clever piece of code that is nearly impossible for others to understand is not good code, it is actually bad code, because programmers often work in teams and other team members should be able to read your code and understand it easily instead of having to waste many minutes trying to decipher what the code is doing. The above is not too bad because what it is doing is relatively simple. But the more complicated the code is, the better it is to break it up into multiple lines to make it easier to understand.

Moving on, below we use the **capitalizeFirstLetter()** function twice in the same statement on lines 8 and 9 in order to capitalize the first letters of both the **first_name** and the **second_name** variables, so that each of "james" and "potter" becomes "James" and "Potter":

```
 1 ▾ <script>
 2 ▾     function capitalizeFirstLetter(word) {
 3             return word[0].toUpperCase() + word.substring(1, word.length);
 4         }
 5
 6         var first_name = 'james';
 7         var second_name = 'potter';
 8         document.write(capitalizeFirstLetter(first_name)
 9             + ' ' + capitalizeFirstLetter(second_name));
10     </script>
```

James Potter

Below we have a different example:

```
 1 ▾ <script>
 2 ▾     function capitalizeFirstLetter(word) {
 3             return word[0].toUpperCase() + word.substring(1, word.length);
 4         }
 5
 6         var full_name = 'james potter';
 7         document.write(capitalizeFirstLetter(full_name));
 8     </script>
```

James potter

Above, only "james" ends up being capitalized because we are passing the "james potter" string all in one go to the **capitalizeFirstLetter()** function. The function capitalizes the first letter and returns everything after it unchanged. It does not care about any spaces there might be in the string, so we end up with "James potter".

8. Arrays

We have already spoken of data types. We have strings, numbers and booleans. In this chapter we will cover a new data type known as an array.

If you think of an ordinary variable as a box that holds things, an array is a box that holds other boxes, which in turn hold things.

Below, we have declared an array named **fruits** with two string values inside it. An array is declared using square brackets **[ ]**.

```
i 1 ▾ <script>
  2      var fruits = ['apple', 'orange'];
  3   </script>
```

As can be seen on line 2, the two values placed inside the array are separated by a comma.

Below we access the values we placed inside the fruits array:

```
i 1 ▾ <script>                                      apple
  2      var fruits = ['apple', 'orange'];          orange
  3      document.write(fruits[0]);
  4      document.write('<br>');
  5      document.write(fruits[1]);
  6   </script>
```

We already discussed the way you can access the first character of a string variable using **[0]**, and the other characters using their appropriate index values. Arrays, like strings, can be accessed using similar index values. Above, on line 3 we write out the contents of **fruits[0]**, which means "the value that is at index 0 of the array". The result is that the word "apple" gets printed out. On line 5 we write out the word "orange" using **fruits[1]**, because "orange" is at index 1.

Below I have added another value to the array on line 3, writing it out on line 8:

```
i  1 ▾ <script>
   2 ▾     var fruits = ['apple', 'orange',
   3             'banana'];
   4         document.write(fruits[0]);
   5         document.write('<br>');
   6         document.write(fruits[1]);
   7         document.write('<br>');
   8         document.write(fruits[2]);
   9    </script>
```
apple
orange
banana

Since 'banana' is at index 2, we use **fruits[2]** to access it online 8. It is unnatural and confusing to use the number 2 to access the *third* item in the array, this is something you just have to get used to. This leads to mistakes even among experienced programmers when they do not pay sufficient attention to the code they are writing.

Instead of printing out each value on a separate line of code, we can use a **for** loop to do the job for us in a few lines of code regardless of how long the array is:

```
i  1 ▾ <script>
   2 ▾     var fruits = ['apple', 'orange',
   3             'banana'];
   4 ▾     for(var i = 0; i < fruits.length; i++) {
   5             document.write(fruits[i]);
   6             document.write('<br>');
   7         }
   8    </script>
```
apple
orange
banana

On line 4 we declare that the **for** loop should run as long as **i** is less then **fruits.length**. The **length** attribute returns the number of items in the array. If we were dealing with a string, **length** would return how many characters were inside the string. Below I have added a new statement on lines 5-7 that prints out the length of the array in the preview area:

```
i  1 ▾ <script>
   2 ▾     var fruits = ['apple', 'orange',
   3             'banana'];
   4
   5         document.write('length of fruits '
   6             + 'array is: ' + fruits.length +
   7             '<br>');
   8
   9 ▾     for(var i = 0; i < fruits.length; i++) {
  10             document.write(fruits[i]);
  11             document.write('<br>');
  12         }
  13    </script>
```
length of fruits array is: 3
apple
orange
banana

In the **for** loop, since **fruits.length** is 3, the result is that we are practically telling the loop to run as long as the variable **i** is less than three. Since **i** starts at zero (because we wrote **var i = 0** in the loop's condition), this means that the loop will run three times. Each time, it will increase **i** by one (because we wrote **i++** in the loop condition), and once it becomes three, the condition **i < fruits.length** ends up being false, so that loop ends. To illustrate, below on line 6 we print out the value of **i** during every loop:

```
 1   <script>
 2       var fruits = ['apple', 'orange',
 3           'banana'];
 4
 5       for(var i = 0; i < fruits.length; i++) {
 6           document.write('i is ' + i + '<br>');
 7           document.write(fruits[i]);
 8           document.write('<br>');
 9       }
10   </script>
```

```
i is 0
apple
i is 1
orange
i is 2
banana
```

Once the value of **i** becomes 3, the condition **i < fruits.length** becomes false, since **i** will not be less than 3, it will be *equal to* 3.

Now, if we add many new items to the array, they will all get printed out without us having to make changes to the **for** loop:

```
 1   <script>
 2       var fruits = ['apple', 'orange',
 3           'banana', 'lemon', 'strawberry',
 4           'mango', 'blackberry'];
 5
 6       for(var i = 0; i < fruits.length; i++) {
 7           document.write('i is ' + i + '<br>');
 8           document.write(fruits[i]);
 9           document.write('<br>');
10       }
11   </script>
12
13
14
15
16
17
18
19
```

```
i is 0
apple
i is 1
orange
i is 2
banana
i is 3
lemon
i is 4
strawberry
i is 5
mango
i is 6
blackberry
```

Above, on lines 3 and 4 we have added four new fruits to the **fruits** array, but on lines 6-10 we have the same loop as before. Since we have made the array larger, **fruits.length** now equals 7. This means that the loop will run seven times since on line 6, inside the loop condition, we are saying the loop should run as long as **i** is less than **fruits.length**, whatever **fruits.length** might be. Any items we add or remove from the array affect the value of **fruits.length**, which affects how many times the loop will run.

Array functions

Similar to strings, arrays have numerous functions that help programmers operate on them. The first function we will discuss is the **toString()** function[4] which prints out everything inside the array as a string. This can be useful when you are not sure what is inside the array and you want to quickly take a look at its contents. Below we have an array named **car_makers**, which contains the names of three car companies.

```
i  1 ▾ <script>
   2 ▾     var car_makers = ['Toyota', 'Ford',
   3           'Tesla'];
   4
   5         document.write(car_makers.toString());
   6   </script>
```

Toyota,Ford,Tesla

Above, on line 5, we use **car_makers.toString()** to get the all of the contents of the array as one string.

Below, on lines 6 and 7 I add two new statements. The first one simply prints out the length of the array, which is 3. The second statement, however, prints out the length of the string returned by **.toString()**, which is 17.

```
i  1 ▾ <script>
   2 ▾     var car_makers = ['Toyota', 'Ford',
   3           'Tesla'];
   4
   5         document.write(car_makers.toString() + '<br>');
   6         document.write(car_makers.length + '<br>');
   7         document.write(car_makers.toString().length);
   8   </script>
```

Toyota,Ford,Tesla
3
17

The **car_makers.toString().length** statement is known as a "chain". JavaScript starts reading it from left to right. First it gets the array **car_makers**, then it runs the **toString()** function on it. Next, it gets the length attribute of the result of the **toString()** function.

We are telling JavaScript: turn this array into a string, then get the length of the string.

We can even chain multiple functions:

---

[4] The more technically correct name for this type of function is "method". As we have discussed, functions take an input and return a result. Methods, however, *operate on the thing they are called on* and often do not take any inputs and sometimes do not return any outputs. To avoid over-complicating the matter I will continue referring to the as functions.

```
i  1▾ <script>
   2▾     var car_makers = ['Toyota', 'Ford',
   3           'Tesla'];
   4
   5       document.write(car_makers.toString() + '<br>');
   6       document.write(car_makers.length + '<br>');
   7       document.write(car_makers.toString().toUpperCase());
   8  </script>
```

Toyota.Ford.Tesla
3
TOYOTA.FORD.TESLA

Above, on line 7, we first turn **car_makers** into a string, then use **toUpperCase()** to turn the string into an all-caps string.

Below, we go further, using the **substring()** string function to only get the word "TOYOTA":

```
i  1▾ <script>
   2▾     var car_makers = ['Toyota', 'Ford',
   3           'Tesla'];
   4
   5       document.write(car_makers.toString() + '<br>');
   6       document.write(car_makers.length + '<br>');
   7       document.write(
   8           car_makers.toString().toUpperCase().substring(0,6)
   9           );
  10  </script>
```

Toyota.Ford.Tesla
3
TOYOTA

On line 8, we use the **substring()** function (covered in the chapter on strings) to extract everything in the string at indexes 0 to 6, which happens to be the word "TOYOTA".

Note that the only reason we are able to use string functions like **toUpperCase()** and **substring()** on the **car_makers** array is that we are first converting it to a string using **toString()**. Without **toString()**, using string functions on an array would lead to an error.

Back to array functions, the next function we will discuss is the **push()** function. This function allows us to push an element onto the end of an array, as follows:

```
i  1▾ <script>
   2▾     var car_makers = ['Toyota', 'Ford',
   3           'Tesla'];
   4       document.write(car_makers.length + '<br>');
   5       car_makers.push('BMW');
   6       document.write(car_makers.length + '<br>');
   7       document.write(car_makers.toString());
   8  </script>
```

3
4
Toyota.Ford.Tesla.BMW

On line 3 above we print out the length of the array, which is 3, since it begins with three elements. On line 4 we use the **push()** function to add a new element to the array, which is the string **BMW**. When we print out the array's length again on line 6, this time the length is 4, because we have added a new element to the array. On line 7 we use **toString()** to print out all of the array's contents, which now has **BMW** at the end.

The opposite of the **push()** function is the **pop()** function, which causes the last element of the array to be "popped" out.

```
i  1 ▾ <script>
   2 ▾     var car_makers = ['Toyota', 'Ford',
   3             'Tesla'];
   4         var last_element = car_makers.pop();
   5         document.write(last_element);
   6         document.write('<br>');
   7         document.write(car_makers.toString());
   8  </script>
```

Tesla
Toyota,Ford

On line 4, we create a new variable **last_element** and put the result of **car_makers.pop()** inside it. When we print out the value of **last_element** on line 5, we see that the word "Tesla" is printed out in the preview area.

On line 7 we have something interesting. When we print out the array's contents, we see only Toyota and Ford. The array now has only two elements. This is because the **pop()** function does two things at the same time: it returns the last element of the array, *and* it removes that element from the array.

Below, we use a **while** loop to pop out every element of the array:

```
i  1 ▾ <script>
   2 ▾     var car_makers = ['Toyota', 'Ford',
   3             'Tesla'];
   4         document.write('The length of the '
   5         + ' array before the loop is: '
   6         + car_makers.length + '<br>');
   7
   8 ▾     while(car_makers.length > 0) {
   9             document.write(car_makers.pop()
  10             + '<br>');
  11             document.write('Length now: '
  12             + car_makers.length + '<br>');
  13         }
  14
  15         document.write('The length of the '
  16         + ' array at the end of the loop: '
  17         + car_makers.length);
  18  </script>
```

The length of the array before the loop is: 3
Tesla
Length now: 2
Ford
Length now: 1
Toyota
Length now: 0
The length of the array at the end of the loop: 0

On lines 4-6, we print out the starting length of the array, which is 3. Inside the **while** loop, the condition we have is **car_makers.length > 0**, which means that the loop should run as long as the length of the **car_makers** array is greater than zero, meaning as long as it is non-empty. On line 9, we have **document.write(car_makers.pop())**. This pops out the last element of the array and immediately passes it to the **document.write()** function, so that it ends up being printed out. On lines 11-12 we print out the new length of the array, which as you can see in the preview area keeps going down during every loop. Once the loop is finished, the length of the array is zero.

We can even use **pop()** to remove elements from an array without doing anything with the popped out element, as follows:

```
1 ▾ <script>
2 ▾     var car_makers = ['Toyota', 'Ford',
3           'Tesla'];
4 ▾     while(car_makers.length > 0) {
5           car_makers.pop();
6       }
7
8       document.write(car_makers.toString());
9   </script>
```

Above, the loop on lines 4-6 removes all the elements of the array. When we try to print out the contents of the array using **toString()** on line 8, nothing is printed out because the array has nothing in it anymore.

An alternative to **push()** is **unshift()**, which adds an element to the *beginning* of an array rather than to its end:

```
1 ▾ <script>
2 ▾     var car_makers = ['Toyota', 'Ford',
3           'Tesla'];
4       car_makers.push('BMW');
5       document.write(car_makers.toString()
6         + '<br>');
7
8       car_makers.unshift('KIA');
9       document.write(car_makers.toString());
10  </script>
```

Toyota,Ford,Tesla,BMW
KIA,Toyota,Ford,Tesla,BMW

Above, on line 4 we use the already-covered **push()** function to add **BMW** as the final element of the **car_makers** array. We then print out the result on lines 5-6. Next, on line 8 we use **unshift()** to add **KIA** as the first element of the array. On printing out the array on line 9, we now see that **KIA** is the first element of the array (second line of the preview).

Do not worry about memorizing the names of these functions. Even experienced programmers have to look them up at times. What is important is to know such functions exist, it is then easy to find them by doing an internet search. For example you can search "javascript remove last item of array" or "javascript add item to beginning of array" and you will find dozens of websites that mention the relevant functions.

What if for some reason we wanted to move the last element of an array to the beginning? We can do that by using **pop()** and **unshift()** together:

```
i  1▾  <script>
   2▾      var car_makers = ['Toyota', 'Ford',
   3              'Tesla'];
   4          car_makers.unshift(car_makers.pop());
   5          document.write(car_makers.toString());
   6  </script>
```

Tesla,Toyota,Ford

Above, on line 4 we are using **car_makers.pop()** to pop out the last element, but since we are doing it inside the brackets of **car_makers.unshift()**, the popped out element ends up inside the array but at the beginning, as seen in the preview. If you are a bit confused by this, we can break it down into more steps to make it clearer:

```
i  1▾  <script>
   2▾      var car_makers = ['Toyota', 'Ford',
   3              'Tesla'];
   4          var last_element = car_makers.pop();
   5          car_makers.unshift(last_element);
   6          document.write(car_makers.toString());
   7  </script>
```

Tesla,Toyota,Ford

The above code does exactly the same thing as before. On line 4 we pop out the last element and put it inside a variable. Then on line 5 we put the value of this variable into the array as its first element. Instead of using the **last_element** variable as an intermediary, we could simply write **car_makers.unshift(car_makers.pop())** to capture the result of **car_makers.pop()** and put it back into the array in one step instead of two.

We also have the **shift()** function which like pop() removes items from the array, but unlike **pop()** it removes from the front of the array rather than the end.

Deconstructing Shakespeare

In this section, we deconstruct a Shakespeare verse from Sonnet 130 and introduce some new operations in the process.

```
i  1▾  <script>
   2          var verse = "I love to hear her speak,"
   3              + " yet well I know "
   4              + "That music hath a far more "
   5              + "pleasing sound;";
   6
   7          document.write(verse);
   8  </script>
```

I love to hear her speak, yet well I know That music hath a far more pleasing sound;

Above, we first have a very long string in which I have placed the verse. The verse is made up of two lines in the original, as follows:

> I love to hear her speak, yet well I know
> That music hath a far more pleasing sound;

But to simplify the example, I have turned the verse into one very long string. In the preview area you see the verse broken into three lines simply because there is not enough space to show it all on one line. If I make my browser window larger, the preview area expands and the browser tries to show all of the verse on one line (I have also zoomed out the browser text in order to get a screenshot that would fit within a book):

> I love to hear her speak, yet well I know That music hath a far more pleasing sound;

The split() function

Back to the business at hand, below I use a new string function called **split()** to split the string and make an array out of it:

```
1  <script>
2      var verse = "I love to hear her speak,"
3          + " yet well I know "
4          + "That music hath a far more "
5          + "pleasing sound;";
6
7      var verse_words = verse.split(" ");
8      document.write(verse_words[1]);
9  </script>
```

love

On line 7, **verse.split(" ")** tells JavaScript to split the string at every space. This means that JavaScript creates a new array with the word "I" as its first element, the word "love" as the second element, "to" as the third element, "hear" as the fourth element, and so on. The stuff between the two quotation marks is what JavaScript will split the string at, at present we have placed a space between the quotation marks. On line 8, we print out the *second* item of the result stored in the **verse_words** variable, which is the word "love".

Below I print out the contents of the **verse_words** array using the **toString()** function:

```
i  1 ▾ <script>
   2       var verse = "I love to hear her speak,"
   3           + " yet well I know "
   4           + "That music hath a far more "
   5           + "pleasing sound;";
   6
   7       var verse_words = verse.split(" ");
   8       document.write(verse_words.toString());
   9  </script>
```

I.love.to.hear.her.speak..yet.well.I.know.

Above, the entire array is printed out on one line. Since there isn't enough space available to see the whole line, we can only see until "know".

Below I use a **for** loop to print out all of the contents of the **verse_words** array, with each array element on its own line:

```
i  1 ▾ <script>
   2       var verse = "I love to hear her speak,"
   3           + " yet well I know "
   4           + "That music hath a far more "
   5           + "pleasing sound;";
   6
   7       var verse_words = verse.split(" ");
   8       for(var i = 0; i < verse_words.length;
   9 ▾     i++) {
  10         document.write(verse_words[i]);
  11         document.write('<br>');
  12       }
  13  </script>
  14
  15
  16
  17
  18
  19
  20
  21
  22
  23
  24
```

I
love
to
hear
her
speak,
yet
well
I
know
That
music
hath
a
far
more
pleasing
sound;

A new type of for loop

We can now introduce a new type of loop that is often useful when going over an array. This loop is also a **for** loop, but it uses a special syntax in the conditional:

```
i  1 ▾ <script>
   2       var verse = "I love to hear her speak,"
   3           + " yet well I know "
   4           + "That music hath a far more "
   5           + "pleasing sound;";
   6
   7       var verse_words = verse.split(" ");
   8 ▾     for(var i in verse_words) {
   9          document.write(verse_words[i]);
  10          document.write('<br>');
  11       }
  12   </script>
```

I
love
to
hear
her
speak,
yet
well
I

The above loop does exactly the same thing as the earlier loop. You can think of it as something of a shorthand that is easier to type. The meaning of **for (var i in verse_words)** is: "for each element in **verse_words**, do the following, while using **i** to represent the index value of the current element".

Catching words

We are now ready to perform operations on the **verse_words** array. Below, I have updated the loop to print out words starting with "h":

```
i  1 ▾ <script>
   2       var verse = "I love to hear her speak,"
   3           + " yet well I know "
   4           + "That music hath a far more "
   5           + "pleasing sound;";
   6
   7       var verse_words = verse.split(" ");
   8
   9 ▾     for(var i in verse_words) {
  10          var current_word = verse_words[i];
  11          if(current_word[0] === 'h' ||
  12 ▾          current_word[0] === 'H') {
  13             document.write(current_word);
  14             document.write('<br>');
  15          }
  16       }
  17   </script>
```

hear
her
hath

On line 10, I put the current array element into a new variable named **current_word**. On lines 11-12, I check whether the first letter of **current_word** is a lowercase or uppercase "h". **current_word[0]** means "the first character of the string" when we are dealing with a string, as has been covered before.

On lines 11-12 we need to do two checks rather than one because in JavaScript an "h" is different from an "H". If we had only written **if(current_word[0] === 'h')**, this would not have caught any words starting with an "H". The condition therefore says: "If the word's first character is a lower case "h", OR if it is an uppercase "H", then do this".

As can be seen in the preview area, the loop detected three words that started with an "h".

The charAt() function

Programmers generally reserve accessing variables by index (as in **my_var[0]**) for arrays. It is confusing and unusual to use it on a string. We have done it so far for simplicity's sake. The better and safer method is to use the **charAt()** string function, as follows:

```
1  <script>
2      var verse = "I love to hear her speak,"
3          + " yet well I know "
4          + "That music hath a far more "
5          + "pleasing sound;";
6
7      var verse_words = verse.split(" ");
8
9      for(var i in verse_words) {
10         var current_word = verse_words[i];
11         var first_letter = current_word.charAt(0);
12         if(first_letter === 'h' ||
13             first_letter === 'H') {
14             document.write(current_word);
15             document.write('<br>');
16         }
17     }
18 </script>
```

hear
her
hath

Above, on line 11 I create a new variable named **first_letter**. I use **current_word.chartAt(0)** to extract the first character of **current_word**. The zero refers to index 0 of the string.

We can simplify the **if** statement as follows:

```
i  1▾ <script>
   2       var verse = "I love to hear her speak,"
   3           + " yet well I know "
   4           + "That music hath a far more "
   5           + "pleasing sound;";
   6
   7       var verse_words = verse.split(" ");
   8
   9▾      for(var i in verse_words) {
  10           var current_word = verse_words[i];
  11           var first_letter = current_word.charAt(0);
  12           first_letter = first_letter.toLowerCase();
  13▾          if(first_letter === 'h') {
  14               document.write(current_word);
  15               document.write('<br>');
  16           }
  17       }
  18  </script>
```
hear
her
hath

On line 12, I use **toLowerCase()** to convert **first_letter** to a lower case letter. Now a single check on line 13 is sufficient: we only need to check for "h" rather than having to check for "H". Regardless of whether the first letter is "h" or "H", since we are forcing it to always become an "h" on line 12, on line 13 we only need to check for lowercase "h". We *never* run into an uppercase "H" on line 13 because line 12 prevents that.

Instead of doing **toLowerCase()** on its own line, we can do it right inside the **if** statement:

```
i  1▾ <script>
   2       var verse = "I love to hear her speak,"
   3           + " yet well I know "
   4           + "That music hath a far more "
   5           + "pleasing sound;";
   6
   7       var verse_words = verse.split(" ");
   8
   9▾      for(var i in verse_words) {
  10           var current_word = verse_words[i];
  11           var first_letter = current_word.charAt(0);
  12▾          if(first_letter.toLowerCase() === 'h') {
  13               document.write(current_word);
  14               document.write('<br>');
  15           }
  16       }
  17  </script>
```
hear
her
hath

Above on line 12 **first_letter.toLowerCase()** forces every first letter to become lowercase right before the comparison.

We can even do away with **first_letter** variable, as follows:

```
i   1 ▾ <script>
    2       var verse = "I love to hear her speak,"          hear
    3           + " yet well I know "                         her
    4           + "That music hath a far more "               hath
    5           + "pleasing sound;";
    6
    7       var verse_words = verse.split(" ");
    8
    9 ▾     for(var i in verse_words) {
   10           var current_word = verse_words[i];
   11           if(current_word.charAt(0).toLowerCase()
   12 ▾             === 'h') {
   13               document.write(current_word);
   14               document.write('<br>');
   15           }
   16       }
   17   </script>
```

On line 11, we do everything in one step. We get the first letter of **current_word** using **charAt()**, then we immediately turn it to lower case, then we compare it to "h".

We can even go further by eliminating the **current_word** variable, as follows:

```
i   1 ▾ <script>
    2       var verse = "I love to hear her speak,"          hear
    3           + " yet well I know "                         her
    4           + "That music hath a far more "               hath
    5           + "pleasing sound;";
    6
    7       var verse_words = verse.split(" ");
    8
    9 ▾     for(var i in verse_words) {
   10           if(verse_words[i].charAt(0).toLowerCase()
   11 ▾             === 'h') {
   12               document.write(verse_words[i]);
   13               document.write('<br>');
   14           }
   15       }
   16   </script>
```

Now on line 10 we get the current array element of **verse_words** using **verse_words[i]**, then we get its first character using **chartAt(0)**, then we convert it to lowercase, then we do the comparison, all inside the **if** statement's condition.

The above code is terser and cleverer, but it is not necessarily better. Sometimes it is better to use an intermediate variable (such as **current_word**), which makes it easier to understand the code. Right now a reader has to spend a while looking at line 10 before they understand what is going on. By using intermediate variables like **current_word** and **first_letter**, we make it easier for humans to understand it, even if it makes no difference to the end result.

When reading code written by experienced programmers you often run into examples like line 10 above, where multiple operations are chained together. Unless you have spent a lot of time reading and writing code, it is natural for these chains to be confusing and difficult to understand.

Nested loops

Below, we have a new piece of code that finds every word that contains the letter "i" or "I" at any point (not just the beginning of the word):

```
1   <script>
2       var verse = "I love to hear her speak,"
3           + " yet well I know "
4           + "That music hath a far more "
5           + "pleasing sound;";
6
7       var verse_words = verse.split(" ");
8
9       for(var i in verse_words) {
10          var current_word = verse_words[i];
11          for(var j = 0; j < current_word.length;j++)
12          {
13              current_letter = current_word.charAt(j);
14              current_letter = current_letter.toLowerCase();
15              if(current_letter === 'i') {
16                  document.write(current_word);
17                  document.write('<br>');
18              }
19          }
20      }
21  </script>
```

```
I
I
music
pleasing
```

We have a nested loop above, meaning one loop inside another. First we loop over all of the array elements, and inside of that, we loop over every character of every word. The first thing to notice is that on line 11, we are using **j** inside the inner for loop rather than **i**, because the variable name **i** is already being used by the outer loop. Using the same variable name in both loops would not make sense and would lead to errors.

In order to make it easier to understand what is going on in the code, below I have added some extra **document.write()** statements:

```
i   1▾  <script>
    2       var verse = "I love to hear her speak,"
    3           + " yet well I know "
    4           + "That music hath a far more "
    5           + "pleasing sound;";
    6
    7       var verse_words = verse.split(" ");
    8
    9▾      for(var i in verse_words) {
   10           var current_word = verse_words[i];
   11           document.write('Currently at word: ' + current_word);
   12           document.write('<br>');
   13           for(var j = 0; j < current_word.length;j++)
   14▾          {
   15               current_letter = current_word.charAt(j);
   16               current_letter = current_letter.toLowerCase();
   17               document.write(current_letter + ' / ');
   18▾              if(current_letter === 'i') {
   19                   document.write('<br>Found an i in the word: ');
   20                   document.write(current_word);
   21               }
   22           }
   23           document.write('<br>');
   24       }
   25  </script>
```

Here is a sample of the result in the preview area:

```
Currently at word: I
i /
Found an i in the word: I
Currently at word: love
l / o / v / e /
Currently at word: to
t / o /
Currently at word: hear
h / e / a / r /
Currently at word: her
h / e / r /
Currently at word: speak,
s / p / e / a / k / , /
Currently at word: yet
y / e / t /
Currently at word: well
w / e / l / l /
Currently at word: I
i /
Found an i in the word: I
Currently at word: know
```

In the outer loop we print out which word we are currently processing (on line 11). In the inner loop, we print out each letter we are processing followed by a slash, in order to separate it from the letter that comes after it. If the inner loop finds any occurrences of the letter "i", it prints out "Found an i..." on line 19. Once the inner loop is done, we print out a new line on line 23.

At that point, the code goes back to the top of the outer loop, which will process the next word, and so on and so forth.

Notice that on line 15 we wrote **chartAt(j)** rather than **chartAt(0)** because **j** changes with each inner loop, starting at 0 and going up to the final index of the string.

Searching strings with indexOf()

We can accomplish what the previous code did with only one loop by using **indexOf()**. We will first look at a simple example:

```
1 ▾ <script>
2       var verse = "I love to hear her speak,"
3           + " yet well I know "
4           + "That music hath a far more "
5           + "pleasing sound;";
6
7       document.write(verse.indexOf('love'));
8   </script>
```

2

The **indexOf()** function tells us the index of the string we are checking. On line 7, we are requesting the index of the word "love". The result is 2, meaning that the word "love" starts at index 2 of the **verse** variable.

Below I check for the index of the letter "i":

```
1 ▾ <script>
2       var verse = "I love to hear her speak,"
3           + " yet well I know "
4           + "That music hath a far more "
5           + "pleasing sound;";
6
7       document.write(verse.indexOf('i'));
8   </script>
```

50

The result is 50 because this is only searching for lowercase occurrences of "i", which happens to be the "i" in "music".

Back to the previous example where we were checking for words containing "i":

```
i  1▾ <script>
   2      var verse = "I love to hear her speak,"
   3          + " yet well I know "
   4          + "That music hath a far more "
   5          + "pleasing sound;";
   6
   7      var verse_words = verse.split(" ");
   8
   9▾     for(var i in verse_words) {
  10          var current_word = verse_words[i];
  11          current_word = current_word.toLowerCase();
  12▾         if(current_word.indexOf('i') !== -1) {
  13              document.write(current_word);
  14              document.write('<br>');
  15          }
  16      }
  17  </script>
```

```
i
i
music
pleasing
```

Above, I have removed the inner loop and replaced it with an if statement that uses **indexOf()** to check if **current_word** contains an "i" or not. First, on line 11 I turn current_word to lowercase to avoid having to check for both uppercase and lowercase occurrences of the letter "i". On line 12, we have something new. I am checking whether the index of the letter "i" equals -1 or not. That is because **indexOf()** returns the index of the letter if it finds it, but if it does not find it, it returns -1. Here is a simple illustration of this:

```
i  1▾ <script>
   2      document.write("love".indexOf('e'));
   3      document.write("<br>");
   4      document.write("love".indexOf('i'));
   5  </script>
```

```
3
-1
```

Above, on line 2 we print out the index of the letter "e" inside the string "love", which happens to be 3. On line 4 we print out the index of the letter "i". But since the word "love" does not contain the letter "i", .**indexOf()** returns -1. The negative index tells us that **indexOf()** failed to find what we were looking for.

Back to the main example, on line 12 we can check whether current_word contains the letter "i" or not by asking the question: Does the index of "i" inside this variable equal -1 or not? If it equals -1, it means it does not contain an "i", if it does not equal negative one, it contains an "i".

Below is a further illustration:

```
i   1 ▾ <script>
    2       var verse = "I love to hear her speak,"
    3           + " yet well I know "
    4           + "That music hath a far more "
    5           + "pleasing sound;";
    6
    7       var verse_words = verse.split(" ");
    8
    9 ▾     for(var i in verse_words) {
    10          var current_word = verse_words[i];
    11          current_word = current_word.toLowerCase();
    12          document.write(current_word + ' ');
    13          document.write(current_word.indexOf('i'));
    14          document.write('<br>');
    15      }
    16  </script>
    17
    18
    19
    20
    21
    22
    23
    24
```

```
i 0
love -1
to -1
hear -1
her -1
speak, -1
yet -1
well -1
i 0
know -1
that -1
music 3
hath -1
a -1
far -1
more -1
pleasing 5
sound; -1
```

Above, I print out each word along with the index of the letter "i" inside that word. That words that do not contain an "i" all show a negative index, while the ones that contain it either show zero or a positive number.

Joining array elements

We have already covered the **split()** function that turns a string into an array by splitting it up. The **join()** function performs the opposite function. It joins the elements of an array and gives us a string back:

```
i   1 ▾ <script>
    2       var verse = "I love to hear her speak,"
    3           + " yet well I know "
    4           + "That music hath a far more "
    5           + "pleasing sound;";
    6
    7       var verse_words = verse.split(" ");
    8
    9       document.write(verse_words.join(' / '));
    10  </script>
```

```
I / love / to / hear / her /
speak, / yet / well / I / know /
That / music / hath / a / far /
more / pleasing / sound;
```

Above, on line 7 we split the **verse** string in to an array as usual. On line 9, we use **join()** to turn it back into a string. Since the argument to the **join()** function is **' / '**, the array elements are separated by spaces and slashes. This argument could be anything we want. Below I have chosen an asterisk and space:

```
 i  1 ▾ <script>
    2       var verse = "I love to hear her speak,"
    3           + " yet well I know "
    4           + "That music hath a far more "
    5           + "pleasing sound;";
    6
    7       var verse_words = verse.split(" ");
    8
    9       document.write(verse_words.join('* '));
   10   </script>
```

I* love* to* hear* her* speak,* yet* well* I* know* That* music* hath* a* far* more* pleasing* sound;

The argument could even be a **\<br\>** tag to make each array element appear on its own line:

```
 i  1 ▾ <script>
    2       var verse = "I love to hear her speak,"
    3           + " yet well I know "
    4           + "That music hath a far more "
    5           + "pleasing sound;";
    6
    7       var verse_words = verse.split(" ");
    8
    9       document.write(verse_words.join('<br>'));
   10   </script>
   11
   12
   13
   14
   15
```

I
love
to
hear
her
speak,
yet
well
I
know
That

We can also do the splitting and joining on one line as follows:

```
 i  1 ▾ <script>
    2       var verse = "I love to hear her speak,"
    3           + " yet well I know "
    4           + "That music hath a far more "
    5           + "pleasing sound;";
    6
    7       document.write(
    8           verse.split(" ").join(" - ")
    9       );
   10   </script>
```

I - love - to - hear - her - speak, - yet - well - I - know - That - music - hath - a - far - more - pleasing - sound;

Reading line 8 from left to right: we first have the **verse** string variable, then using the **split()** function it is split at the spaces into an array, next using the **join()** function it is joined back together into a string with the array elements separated by spaces and dashes.

Analyzing students' names

In this example, we have the first and last names of 14 students in an array. Our task is to find out the master common first names among them. Writing a program to analyze a mere 14 names is unnecessary, but imagine working for the census office and having to analyze millions of names. That is when programming skills are indispensable.

```
i  1 ▾ <script>
   2       var student_names =
   3 ▾         ['Sophia Johnson', 'Noah Smith', 'Emma Davis',
   4             'Liam Williams', 'Mason Brown', 'Ava Garcia',
   5             'Jacob Jones', 'William Miller', 'Liam Anderson',
   6             'Olivia Wilson', 'Emma Jacobson', 'Olivia Young',
   7             'Liam Wright', 'Sophia Baker'];
```

In order to proceed with our analysis, we first create a new array **first_names** that will only hold the first names (line 8 below).

```
i  1 ▾ <script>
   2       var student_names =
   3 ▾         ['Sophia Johnson', 'Noah Smith', 'Emma Davis',
   4             'Liam Williams', 'Mason Brown', 'Ava Garcia',
   5             'Jacob Jones', 'William Miller', 'Liam Anderson',
   6             'Olivia Wilson', 'Emma Jacobson', 'Olivia Young',
   7             'Liam Wright', 'Sophia Baker'];
   8       var first_names = [];
```

Below is the loop we will use to go over the names:

```
i  1 ▾ <script>
   2       var student_names =
   3 ▾         ['Sophia Johnson', 'Noah Smith', 'Emma Davis',
   4             'Liam Williams', 'Mason Brown', 'Ava Garcia',
   5             'Jacob Jones', 'William Miller', 'Liam Anderson',
   6             'Olivia Wilson', 'Emma Jacobson', 'Olivia Young',
   7             'Liam Wright', 'Sophia Baker'];
   8       var first_names = [];
   9 ▾   for(var i in student_names) {
  10         student_full_name = student_names[i];
  11         document.write('current name: ' + student_full_name);
  12         document.write('<br>');
  13         student_split_name = student_full_name.split(' ');
  14         document.write('split name: ' + student_split_name.toString());
  15         document.write('<br>');
  16         student_first_name = student_split_name[0];
  17         document.write('first name only: ' + student_first_name);
  18         document.write('<br>');
  19         first_names.push(student_first_name);
  20     }
```

Seeing all of that code in one loop can be a little overwhelming, but there is actually nothing new in it that we have not already covered. I have added **document.write()** statements in various places in order to show what is going on inside the loop. Here is what gets printed out in the preview area:

```
current name: Sophia Johnson
split name: Sophia,Johnson
first name only: Sophia
current name: Noah Smith
split name: Noah,Smith
first name only: Noah
current name: Emma Davis
split name: Emma,Davis
first name only: Emma
current name: Liam Williams
split name: Liam,Williams
first name only: Liam
current name: Mason Brown
split name: Mason,Brown
first name only: Mason
current name: Ava Garcia
split name: Ava,Garcia
first name only: Ava
current name: Jacob Jones
split name: Jacob,Jones
first name only: Jacob
```

Try to read the code to see if you can understand everything that is going on before I explain it below.

Below is the loop with the **document.write()** statements removed:

```
 9 ▾    for(var i in student_names) {
10          student_full_name = student_names[i];
11          student_split_name = student_full_name.split(' ');
12          student_first_name = student_split_name[0];
13          first_names.push(student_first_name);
14      }
```

On line 10 we place the current student's name in the **student_full_name** variable. On line 11 we split this variable at the spaces and place the result inside the array variable **student_split_name**. On line 12, we get the first element of the **student_split_name** array using the zero index and place it inside the **student_first_name** string variable. On line 13 we use the **push()** function to place the value of this variable inside the **first_names** array.

Below I use **document.write()** and **toString()** to print out the contents of the **first_names** array after the loop is done:

```
9 ▾    for(var i in student_names) {
10         student_full_name = student_names[i];
11         student_split_name = student_full_name.split(' ');
12         student_first_name = student_split_name[0];
13         first_names.push(student_first_name);
14     }
15     document.write(first_names.toString());
```

Here is the result:

> Sophia,Noah,Emma,Liam,Mason,Ava,Jacob,William,Liam,

There is more inside the array than can be seen above since the preview area is not large enough to show all of the contents. Below on line 15 we use **join()** rather than **toString()** to turn the **first_names** array into a string with the elements separated by spaces and slashes:

```
9 ▾    for(var i in student_names) {
10         student_full_name = student_names[i];
11         student_split_name = student_full_name.split(' ');
12         student_first_name = student_split_name[0];
13         first_names.push(student_first_name);
14     }
15     document.write(first_names.join(' / '));
```

Here is the result:

> Sophia / Noah / Emma / Liam / Mason / Ava / Jacob /
> William / Liam / Olivia / Emma / Olivia / Liam / Sophia

Let us know go on with our analysis. Below we use a new function and a new to proceed with counting the names:

```
15    function countOccurrences(word, array_of_words) {
16        var count = 0;
17        for(var i in array_of_words) {
18            if(word === array_of_words[i]) {
19                count++;
20            }
21        }
22        return count;
23    }
24    for(var i in first_names) {
25        var first_name = first_names[i];
26        var count = countOccurrences(first_name, first_names);
27        document.write(first_name + ' ' + count + '<br>');
28    }
```

Here is the result:

Sophia 2
Noah 1
Emma 2
Liam 3
Mason 1
Ava 1
Jacob 1
William 1
Liam 3
Olivia 2
Emma 2
Olivia 2
Liam 3
Sophia 2

Inside the new loop (lines 24-28) we use the new function **countOccurrences()** to count the number of times each name occurs in the **first_names** array. The **countOccurrences()** function works by going over the **array_of_words** variable that we pass to it and increasing the **count** variable by one each time it detects the value of the **word** variable inside the **array_of_words** array.

Below I have added extra **document.write()** statements to the **countOccurrences()** function in order to show how it works:

```
15 ▾    function countOccurrences(word, array_of_words) {
16          var count = 0;
17          document.write('current word: ' + word + '<br>');
18 ▾        for(var i in array_of_words) {
19              document.write('will compare ' + word +
20                  ' with ' + array_of_words[i] + '<br>');
21
22 ▾            if(word === array_of_words[i]) {
23                  count++;
24                  document.write('match detected!' + '<br>');
25                  document.write('current count: ' + count + '<br>');
26              }
27          }
28          return count;
29      }
```

Here is the output when this function analyzes the name Sophia:

> current word: Sophia
> will compare Sophia with Sophia
> match detected!
> current count: 1
> will compare Sophia with Noah
> will compare Sophia with Emma
> will compare Sophia with Liam
> will compare Sophia with Mason
> will compare Sophia with Ava
> will compare Sophia with Jacob
> will compare Sophia with William
> will compare Sophia with Liam
> will compare Sophia with Olivia
> will compare Sophia with Emma
> will compare Sophia with Olivia
> will compare Sophia with Liam
> will compare Sophia with Sophia
> match detected!
> current count: 2

Back to our analysis, you may have noticed that in the earlier output some names are unnecessarily shown multiple times:

```
Sophia 2
Noah 1
Emma 2
Liam 3
Mason 1
Ava 1
Jacob 1
William 1
Liam 3
Olivia 2
Emma 2
Olivia 2
Liam 3
Sophia 2
```

That is because our new loop at lines 24-28 does not care whether it has already checked the number of occurrences of the name it is seeing. If it sees Sophia multiple times, it will analyze it each time and show its count:

```
24 ▾    for(var i in first_names) {
25           var first_name = first_names[i];
26           var count = countOccurrences(first_name, first_names);
27           document.write(first_name + ' ' + count + '<br>');
28       }
```

Using includes() and the continue statement

We can make the loop smarter by making it avoid re-analyzing names it has already analyzed.

```
24       var analyzed_names = [];
25 ▾    for(var i in first_names) {
26           var first_name = first_names[i];
27           var count = countOccurrences(first_name, first_names);
28           document.write(first_name + ' ' + count + '<br>');
29           analyzed_names.push(first_name);
30       }
```

Above, on line 24 we declare a new array named **analyzed_names**. On line 29 we push each name we analyze inside this array.

Next we add an **if** statement to check whether the name has already been analyzed or not (lines 27-29):

```
24        var analyzed_names = [];
25 ▾      for(var i in first_names) {
26            var first_name = first_names[i];
27 ▾          if(analyzed_names.includes(first_name)) {
28                continue;
29            }
30            var count = countOccurrences(first_name, first_names);
31            document.write(first_name + ' ' + count + '<br>');
32            analyzed_names.push(first_name);
33        }
```

Inside the loop, on line 27 we use a new built-in JavaScript function called **includes()**. This function checks whether an array contains a certain value or not. We are checking if **analyzed_names** contains the **first_name** we are currently analyzing. If it contains it, it means we have already analyzed the name. If so, we want to tell JavaScript to not run the analysis again. In order to do so we use the new **continue** statement on line 28. This statement causes the loop to stop executing and to go back to the top onto the next item. This means that if the name we are checking has already been analyzed previously, the **continue** statement on line 28 causes the statements on lines 30-32 to be ignored.

Here is the result:

Sophia 2
Noah 1
Emma 2
Liam 3
Mason 1
Ava 1
Jacob 1
William 1
Olivia 2

As you can see, there are no duplicate names anymore.

Here is the complete code. I recommend that you read it from top to bottom and try to understand each statement. Reading code and trying to make sense of it is an important part of learning programming:

```
i  1 ▾ <script>
   2       var student_names =
   3 ▾       ['Sophia Johnson', 'Noah Smith', 'Emma Davis',
   4           'Liam Williams', 'Mason Brown', 'Ava Garcia',
   5           'Jacob Jones', 'William Miller', 'Liam Anderson',
   6           'Olivia Wilson', 'Emma Jacobson', 'Olivia Young',
   7           'Liam Wright', 'Sophia Baker'];
   8       var first_names = [];
   9 ▾     for(var i in student_names) {
  10           student_full_name = student_names[i];
  11           student_split_name = student_full_name.split(' ');
  12           student_first_name = student_split_name[0];
  13           first_names.push(student_first_name);
  14       }
  15 ▾     function countOccurrences(word, array_of_words) {
  16           var count = 0;
  17 ▾         for(var i in array_of_words) {
  18 ▾             if(word === array_of_words[i]) {
  19                   count++;
  20               }
  21           }
  22           return count;
  23       }
  24       var analyzed_names = [];
  25 ▾     for(var i in first_names) {
  26           var first_name = first_names[i];
  27 ▾         if(analyzed_names.includes(first_name)) {
  28               continue;
  29           }
  30           var count = countOccurrences(first_name, first_names);
  31           document.write(first_name + ' ' + count + '<br>');
  32           analyzed_names.push(first_name);
  33       }
  34   </script>
```

9. Objects

At this point in this book, you have already mastered the basics of programming. From here on we will discuss more advanced topics that will expose the nitty-gritty of programming to you and will take from a novice to an intermediate learner. Some of the concepts covered from here on are going to be rather advanced and will strongly depend on the things you have already learned. It might be a good idea to review the previous chapters before proceeding.

We have come to the final important data type in JavaScript, objects. Not all languages have this data type. It is, however, one of the most useful data types in JavaScript and it is essential for building large-scale JavaScript programs.

In order to speak about objects, we will start by looking at an example array:

```
i  1 ▾ <script>
   2 ▾     var student_data = ['Sophia Davis', '2', '85220',
   3             'Emma Davis', 'James Davis'];
   4   </script>
```

Above, the **student_data** holds information about a student named Sophia Davis. The problem with this data is that you cannot be exactly sure what the different values stand for. The second element of the array is the number "2", which probably stands for her grade. The next element looks like a ZIP code, and the next two elements look like the student's mother and father names. Now imagine if there were fifty more elements in the array. It could become unmanageably difficult to make sense of the array.

Below is an object named **student_data** that holds the same data as before:

```
i  1 ▾ <script>
   2 ▾     var student_data = {
   3              'full_name' : 'Sophia Davis',
   4              'grade' : '2',
   5              'zip_code' : '85220',
   6              'mother_full_name' : 'Emma Davis',
   7              'father_full_name' : 'James Davis'
   8          };
   9   </script>
```

Above **student_data** is now an object. Objects are declared using curly braces **{}**. An object is made up of what are known as key-value pairs. They key "full_name" is associated with the value "Sophia Davis".

Both arrays and objects are like tables, but with a crucial difference. An array is like a table with numbers as its first column. You find each item by looking up its number:

student_data = [

0	'Sophia Davis',
1	'2',
2	'85220',
3	'Emma Davis',
4	'James Davis'

];

But an object is like a table with descriptive labels as its first column rather than numbers, making it possible to look up each value by a label (or key) rather than a number:

student_data = {

'full_name'	'Sophia Davis',
'grade'	'2',
'zip_code'	'85220',
'mother_full_name'	'Emma Davis',
'father_full_name'	'James Davis'

};

Below is an example of accessing an object's value by a key:

```
i   1 ▾ <script>
    2 ▾    var student_data = {
    3          'full_name' : 'Sophia Davis',
    4          'grade' : '2',
    5          'zip_code' : '85220',
    6          'mother_full_name' : 'Emma Davis',
    7          'father_full_name' : 'James Davis'
    8       };
    9       document.write(student_data.full_name);
   10 </script>
```
Sophia Davis

On line 9, using the statement **student_data.full_name**, we access the value we associated with the **full_name** key on line 3. The key-value pair is called a "property". For example we say that **full_name** is a property of the **student_data** object whose key is **full_name** and whose value is "Sophia Davis".

Objects can be nested, which allows us to create highly readable and useful ways of representing our data:

```
i   1 ▾ <script>
    2 ▾    var student_data = {
    3          'full_name' : 'Sophia Davis',
    4          'grade' : '2',
    5          'zip_code' : '85220',
    6 ▾        'mother' : {
    7              'full_name' : 'Emma Davis',
    8              'phone_number' : '12345678',
    9          },
   10 ▾        'father' : {
   11              'full_name' : 'James Davis',
   12              'phone_number' : '23456789',
   13          }
   14       };
   15       document.write(student_data.mother.full_name);
   16 </script>
```
Emma Davis

Above, I have removed the **mother_full_name** key. Instead, we now have a **mother** key that refers to a new object with two keys, **full_name** and **phone_number**. It is the same for the father's data. On line 15 I use **student_data.mother.full_name** to get the student's mother's full name.

Another way to declare objects is to declare an empty object then add stuff to it later on:

```
i   1 ▾ <script>
    2       var student = {};
    3       student.full_name = 'Liam Smith';
    4       student.father = {};
    5       student.father.full_name = 'Jeffrey Smith';
    6       document.write(student.father.full_name);
    7 </script>
```
Jeffrey Smith

Above, note that only the **student** variable needs to be declared with a **var**. The rest of the declarations do not need a **var**.

Below we have an object variable named city that represents the city of Ann Arbor in Michigan:

```
i  1 ▾ <script>
   2        var city = {};
   3        city.name = 'Ann Arbor';
   4        city.county = 'Washtenaw';
   5        city.population = '121000';
   6 ▾      city.zip_codes = [
   7            48103, 48104, 48105, 48106, 48107,
   8            48108, 48109, 48113
   9            ];
```

We use an array to represent the city's eight ZIP codes, meaning that **zip_codes** is an array that is inside the **city** object. We can use this array like any other array, as follows:

```
i  1 ▾ <script>                                          48103
   2        var city = {};                                48104
   3        city.name = 'Ann Arbor';                      48105
   4        city.county = 'Washtenaw';
   5        city.population = '121000';                   48106
   6 ▾      city.zip_codes = [                            48107
   7            48103, 48104, 48105, 48106, 48107,        48108
   8            48108, 48109, 48113                        48109
   9            ];
  10 ▾      for(var i in city.zip_codes) {                48113
  11            document.write(city.zip_codes[i] + '<br>');
  12        }
  13    </script>
```

The above is the same as the below.

```
i  1 ▾ <script>                                          48103
   2        var city = {};                                48104
   3        city.name = 'Ann Arbor';                      48105
   4        city.county = 'Washtenaw';
   5        city.population = '121000';                   48106
   6 ▾      city.zip_codes = [                            48107
   7            48103, 48104, 48105, 48106, 48107,        48108
   8            48108, 48109, 48113                        48109
   9            ];
  10        var zip_codes = city.zip_codes;               48113
  11 ▾      for(var i in zip_codes) {
  12            document.write(zip_codes[i] + '<br>');
  13        }
  14    </script>
```

Above I create a new variable named **zip_codes** on line 10 and put the **city.zip_codes** array inside it, then I use the new **zip_codes** variable inside the loop.

The coffee robot

In this section we will discuss a simple system for communicating with a coffee-making robot using an object. This is something that can actually work in the real world, provided that you have a friend who works as a "back-end" programmer and knows how to write software that can understand requests sent from JavaScript.

We will start by declaring a new object that represents the cup of coffee we want the robot to make:

```
i  1 ▾ <script>
   2       var my_coffee = {};
   3    </script>
```

Next we will declare what kind of cup of coffee we want:

```
i  1 ▾ <script>
   2       var my_coffee = {};
   3 ▾     my_coffee.attributes = {
   4           'origin'  : 'Chiapas',
   5           'organic' : 'Yes',
   6           'grind'   : 'Rough',
   7           'roast'   : 'Medium',
   8           'creamer' : 'None',
   9           'sweetener' : 'None',
  10       };
  11    </script>
```

Next we will declare a function that sends the order to the robot:

```
i  1 ▾ <script>
   2       var my_coffee = {};
   3 ▾     my_coffee.attributes = {
   4           'origin'  : 'Chiapas',
   5           'organic' : 'Yes',
   6           'grind'   : 'Rough',
   7           'roast'   : 'Medium',
   8           'creamer' : 'None',
   9           'sweetener' : 'None',
  10       };
  11 ▾     my_coffee.order = function() {
  12
  13       };
  14    </script>
```

Above I have declared a function named **order** on lines 11-13. As you can see, an object can hold functions. This function can be called by writing **my_coffee.order()**. Note the way we declared the function on line 11, which is different from the way we have done it before. Normally you would write **function order() { }**. But here, we are using a different method of defining functions, which is to declare it "anonymously" (without specifying a name for it) then put it inside a variable, in this case the **my_coffee.order** variable. Even though this function is technically nameless, since we have put it inside a variable, we can use it like any other function by using the variable's name.

The function is at present empty. The first thing we need is a way to access the attributes of the cup of coffee so that we can send them to the robot. In order to do that, we use a new concept known as **this**.

```
11 ▾    my_coffee.order = function() {
12          var cup_properties = this.attributes;
13      };
```

The **this** keyword is used to refer to the current object. When we write **this.attributes** on line 12, JavaScript knows that we mean **my_coffee.attributes** since we are inside a function that is inside this object. Think of **this** as meaning "the current object we are inside of" and it should make sense.

Next we will define the part of the function that actually communicates with the robot, on lines 14-24:

```
11 ▾    my_coffee.order = function() {
12          var cup_properties = this.attributes;
13
14 ▾        $.ajax('http://0.0.0.0/robot/orders', {
15              data: cup_properties,
16 ▾            success: function () {
17                  document.write('The robot successfully '
18                      'received the order!');
19              },
20 ▾            error: function () {
21                  document.write('There was an error '
22                      + 'connecting to the robot');
23              }
24          });
25      };
```

Explaining what is going above is beyond the scope of this book, it is merely there to show readers that JavaScript is not merely a toy, it can actually communicate with real-world machines and control them. What we are doing is sending an "AJAX" request using something called jQuery to the robot's Internet address. On line 15 we have **data: cup_properties**, this means that when we communicate with the robot, we send it the details of the type of cup of coffee we declared earlier. Note that running this code on your local machine will not work since the Internet address defined on line 14 is not a real address.

Above we have only declared the function. If we run the code nothing happens since we are not actually calling the function. The final step would therefore be to call the **order** function:

```
27      my_coffee.order();
28  </script>
```

If everything works correctly, running the code would cause the preview area to show the following message:

The robot successfully received the order!

Text Analyzer

In this section, we will build a simple JavaScript program that we will call Text Analyzer. We will use an object variable named **text_analyzer** to hold the program.[5]

```
i  1▾ <script>
   2▾ var text_analyzer = {
   3       current_text : '',
   4▾      get_words_array : function() {
   5          var text = this.current_text;
   6          var split_text = text.split(' ');
   7          return split_text;
   8      }
   9  };
   10
   11 text_analyzer.current_text =
   12      'And this is Dorlcote Mill. I must '
   13      + 'stand a minute or two here on the bridge '
   14      + 'and look at it, though the clouds are '
   15      + 'threatening, and it is far on in the afternoon. '
   16      + 'Even in this leafless time of departing February '
   17      + 'it is pleasant to look at,-perhaps the chill, '
   18      + 'damp season adds a charm to the trimly kept, '
   19      + 'comfortable dwelling-house, as old as the elms '
   20      + 'and chestnuts that shelter it from the '
   21      + 'northern blast. ';
   22 </script>
```

The **text_analyzer** program currently has only one function named **get_words_array** which splits the string inside **text_analyzer.current_text** and returns the resulting array. On lines 11-21 we place a relatively long string inside

---

[5] Visit my personal website for the code for Text Analyzer and other functions developed throughout this book: http://hawramani.com/?p=66687

text_analyzer.current_text taken from George Eliot's 1860 novel *The Mill on the Floss*.

Notice that when declaring the **get_words_array** on line 4, we are using a colon not an equal sign because we are inside an object and we are declaring the object's keys and values, which are separated by colons. In this case the key is **get_words_array** and the value is an anonymous function.

We will now add a new function to **text_analyzer** that counts the number of words we give the program:

```
i  1 ▾ <script>
   2 ▾ var text_analyzer = {
   3       current_text : '',
   4 ▾     get_words_array : function() {
   5           var text = this.current_text;
   6           var split_text = text.split(' ');
   7           return split_text;
   8       },
   9 ▾     count_words : function() {
  10           return this.get_words_array().length;
  11       }
  12   };
  13
  14   text_analyzer.current_text =
  15       'And this is Dorlcote Mill. I must '
  16       + 'stand a minute or two here on the bridge '
  17       + 'and look at it, though the clouds are '
  18       + 'threatening, and it is far on in the afternoon. '
  19       + 'Even in this leafless time of departing February '
  20       + 'it is pleasant to look at,-perhaps the chill, '
  21       + 'damp season adds a charm to the trimly kept, '
  22       + 'comfortable dwelling-house, as old as the elms '
  23       + 'and chestnuts that shelter it from the '
  24       + 'northern blast. ';
  25   document.write(text_analyzer.count_words());
  26   </script>
```
75

The new function is named **count_words** (lines 9-11). This function makes use of the previously defined function **get_words_array** to get the string as an array, then simply returns the length property of the array. On line 25 we use the **count_words()** function and the result, seen in the preview area, is 75.

To explain what is going on line 10, below I break it down into three lines:

```
   9 ▾     count_words : function() {
  10           var words_array = this.get_words_array();
  11           var length = words_array.length;
  12           return length;
  13       }
```

In the shorter version of the function, writing **this.get_words_array().length** returns the length of the *result* of the **get_words_array()** function. The brackets in **this.get_words_array().length** are crucial. It is a common mistake to forget the brackets so that one writes **this.get_words_array.length**. This leads to a wrong result because JavaScript gets confused into thinking we are trying to get the length of the function's code.

Below are two statements to clarify the issue of the brackets. The first on line 27 uses **count_words** with brackets, while the second one on line 29 does not use the brackets.

```
27    document.write(text_analyzer.count_words());
28    document.write('<br>');
29    document.write(text_analyzer.count_words);
```

Here is the result:

```
75
function () { var words_array =
this.get_words_array(); var length =
words_array.length; return length; }
```

The statement on line 27 works as expected. The statement on line 29, however, returns the function's code. It is the brackets right after the function's name that tells JavaScript to run the function. Without the brackets, JavaScript thinks we are simply referring to the function definition.

Below we add a third function named **get_average_word_length** that analyzes the text to find out the average length of the words in the text.

```
14 ▼    get_average_word_length : function() {
15        var all_word_lengths = 0;
16        var words_array = this.get_words_array();
17 ▼      for(var i in words_array) {
18            var current_word = words_array[i];
19            all_word_lengths = all_word_lengths +
20                current_word.length;
21        }
22        return all_word_lengths / words_array.length;
23      },
24  };
25
26  text_analyzer.current_text =
27      'And this is Dorlcote Mill. I must '
28      + 'stand a minute or two here on the bridge '
29      + 'and look at it, though the clouds are '
30      + 'threatening, and it is far on in the afternoon. '
31      + 'Even in this leafless time of departing February '
32      + 'it is pleasant to look at,-perhaps the chill, '
33      + 'damp season adds a charm to the trimly kept, '
34      + 'comfortable dwelling-house, as old as the elms '
35      + 'and chestnuts that shelter it from the '
36      + 'northern blast. ';
37  document.write(text_analyzer.get_average_word_length());
38  </script>
```

4.386666666666667

In the **get_average_word_length()** function we use **all_word_lengths** to sum up the length of all the words in the text. On line 22 we divide this sum by the number of words in the text to get the average, which as seen in the preview area is 4.386. This average is not fully accurate because our code counts punctuation as part of the word that comes before it. For example "kept," is counted as 5 letters in length. There are ways to fix this but that is a topic for later chapters.

We next add a function for finding out the longest word in the text:

```
24 ▾      get_longest_word : function() {
25            var longest_length_seen_so_far = 0;
26            var longest_word = '';
27            var words_array = this.get_words_array();
28 ▾         for(var i in words_array) {
29                var current_word = words_array[i];
30                if(current_word.length >
31 ▾                 longest_length_seen_so_far) {
32                    longest_word = current_word;
33                    longest_length_seen_so_far =
34                        current_word.length;
35                }
36            }
37            return longest_word;
38        },
39 };
40
41 text_analyzer.current_text =
42        'And this is Dorlcote Mill. I must '
43      + 'stand a minute or two here on the bridge '
44      + 'and look at it, though the clouds are '
45      + 'threatening, and it is far on in the afternoon. '
46      + 'Even in this leafless time of departing February '
47      + 'it is pleasant to look at,-perhaps the chill, '
48      + 'damp season adds a charm to the trimly kept, '
49      + 'comfortable dwelling-house, as old as the elms '
50      + 'and chestnuts that shelter it from the '
51      + 'northern blast. ';
52 document.write(text_analyzer.get_longest_word());
53 </script>
```

dwelling-house.

The **get_longest_word()** function uses what is known as a "high watermark algorithm" to find out the longest word in the text's array of words. In the **for** loop on lines 28-36, each time we see a word that is longer than the ones seen before, we store it in **longest_word** while also storing its length in **longest_length_seen_so_far**. Once the loop is done, **longest_word** ends up containing the longest word in the entire array.

Below I have added a new **document.write()** statement on lines 33-34 to clarify how the **get_longest_word()** function works:

```
24 ▾     get_longest_word : function() {
25           var longest_length_seen_so_far = 0;
26           var longest_word = '';
27           var words_array = this.get_words_array();
28 ▾         for(var i in words_array) {
29               var current_word = words_array[i];
30               if(current_word.length >
31 ▾                 longest_length_seen_so_far) {
32                   longest_word = current_word;
33                   document.write('longest '
34                       + 'word: '
35                       + longest_word + '<br>');
36                   longest_length_seen_so_far =
37                       current_word.length;
38               }
39           }
40           return longest_word;
41       },
```

longest word: And
longest word: this
longest word: Dorlcote
longest word: threatening.
longest word: dwelling-house.
dwelling-house.

As the function runs, at first it considers "And" to be the longest word, since the check **current_word.length > longest_length_seen_so_far** compares 3 with zero. Next time the loop runs it compares the length of "this" with the length of the previously seen "And". Again, since the new word is larger, **longest_word** ends up containing "this". The next word that is checked is the word "is". Since this is shorter than "this", the condition becomes false so that **longest_word** continues to contain "this". In this way each time a word is seen that is longer than the word stored in **longest_word**, **longest_word** is updated to contain the new word. In the end "dwelling-house," wins as the longest word.

Bracket notation and dynamic properties

We have already seen how an object property can be accessed using dot notation, as in **student.full_name**. There is another way of accessing the same property by using bracket notation, as in **student["full_name"]**:

```
i  1 ▾  <script>
   2    var student = {};
   3    student.full_name = "Sophia Davis";
   4    document.write(student.full_name);
   5    document.write('<br>');
   6    document.write(student["full_name"]);
   7    </script>
```

Sophia Davis
Sophia Davis

Above, on line 4 we access the **full_name** property of the **student** object using dot notation, while on line 6 we use bracket notation. The result is the same in both cases.

Below we have an array that contains fruit names. We want to convert this array into an object with the keys as the fruit names and the values as the length of each fruit name:

```
1 <script>
2 var fruits_array = ['banana', 'apple',
3          'orange'];
4
5 </script>
```

Here is an illustration of the object we want to create based on the above array, with each fruit name on the left, and the length of each fruit name on the right as its value:

```
fruits_object = {
    'banana' : 6,
    'apple' : 5,
    'orange' : 6
}
```

Below is the code we use to create just such an object from the array:

```
1 <script>
2 var fruits_array = ['banana', 'apple',
3          'orange'];
4 var fruits_object = {};
5 for(var i in fruits_array) {
6     var current_fruit = fruits_array[i];
7     fruits_object[current_fruit]
8         = current_fruit.length;
9 }
10 </script>
```

Above, we first declare an empty **fruits_object** on line 4. On line 5 we loop over the **fruits_array**. On lines 7-8 is where the interesting stuff happens. By writing fruits_object[current_fruit], we are telling JavaScript to create a property inside the fruits_object that has a key of the value inside **current_fruit**. The first time the loop runs, **fruit_object[current_fruit]** is interpreted by JavaScript as **fruit_object["banana"]**, the second time as **fruit_object["apple"]**, and the third and last time as **fruit_object["orange"]**. These properties do not actually exist inside the object, but by accessing them here and setting them equal to **current_fruit.length**, we create them and put a value inside them all in one step.

You may wonder why instead of using a loop we cannot just write out each property we want to create, as follows:

```
i   1 ▾ <script>
    2 ▾ var fruits_array = ['banana', 'apple',
    3           'orange'];
    4   var fruits_object = {};
    5   fruits_object.banana = "banana".length;
    6   fruits_object.apple = "apple".length;
    7   fruits_object.orange = "orange".length;
    8   </script>
```

The above accomplishes exactly the same thing as before. The difference is that the earlier code can handle arrays of any length. Imagine if **fruits_array** had hundreds of words in it. You would then either have to write a relatively simple loop, or you would have to write a hundred lines to deal with each separate word.

Below we add a new loop to print out the contents of the **fruits_object**:

```
i   1 ▾ <script>
    2 ▾ var fruits_array = ['banana', 'apple',     banana 6
    3           'orange'];                          apple 5
    4   var fruits_object = {};                     orange 6
    5 ▾ for(var i in fruits_array) {
    6       var current_fruit = fruits_array[i];
    7       fruits_object[current_fruit]
    8           = current_fruit.length;
    9   }
   10 ▾ for(var i in fruits_object) {
   11       document.write(i + ' ' +
   12           fruits_object[i]);
   13       document.write('<br>');
   14   }
   15   </script>
```

Above, we have a normal-looking **for** loop on line 10, but this time we are looping over an object not an array. The value of i is not going to be a number, it is going to be one of the keys of the object. The first time the loop runs, **i** contains the word "banana" while **fruits_object[i]** contains the number 6, as if we had an object defined as follows:

```
fruits_object = {
    "banana" : 6
}
```

It can be difficult for even experienced programmers to intuitively make sense of the fact that **i** contains keys and **some_bject[i]** contains values. To avoid confusion, it can help to create variables at the top of the loop with more descriptive names:

```
i   1 ▾ <script>
    2 ▾ var fruits_array = ['banana', 'apple',
    3           'orange'];
    4   var fruits_object = {};
    5 ▾ for(var i in fruits_array) {
    6       var current_fruit = fruits_array[i];
    7       fruits_object[current_fruit]
    8           = current_fruit.length;
    9   }
   10 ▾ for(var i in fruits_object) {
   11       var current_key = i;
   12       var current_value = fruits_object[i];
   13       document.write(current_key);
   14       document.write(' ' + current_value);
   15       document.write('<br>');
   16   }
   17   </script>
```

banana 6
apple 5
orange 6

Printing objects

We cannot use **object.toString()** to print out the contents of an object. Doing so will always cause JavaScript to display **[object Object]** regardless of what the object contains:

```
i   1 ▾ <script>
    2 ▾ var car = {
    3       'maker' : 'Honda',
    4   };
    5   document.write(car.toString());
    6   </script>
```

[object Object]

In this section we will create our own object printing function. The second loop shown earlier already showed how to do this.

```
i   1▾ <script>
    2▾ function print_object(the_object) {
    3▾     document.write('{<br>');
    4▾     for(var i in the_object) {
    5          var key = i;
    6          var value = the_object[i];
    7          document.write('"' + key + '"');
    8          document.write(' : ');
    9          document.write(value);
    10         document.write('<br>');
    11     }
    12     document.write('}<br>');
    13 }
    14
    15▾ var car = {
    16     'maker' : 'Honda',
    17     'year' : '2018',
    18 };
    19 print_object(car);
    20 </script>
```

```
{
"maker" : Honda
"year" : 2018
}
```

Above, the new **print_object** function takes an object and prints out its contents. On line 3 we print out an opening curly brace and a new line. On line 12 we print out a closing curly brace and a new line. These curly braces are not necessary, they are simply for presentation purposes to help a reader immediately know that what is shown is an object's contents. On line 7 we write out **'"' + key + '"'**. This prints out the **key** with a double quotation mark before it and a double quotation mark after it. In the preview area you can see that "maker" and "year" have quotation marks. The strange syntax **'"'** simply means "a string that contains a double quotation mark". The single quotation marks before and after it are used to enclose the string, similar to the way the string **'Apple'** has a single quotation mark before it and after it to tell JavaScript where the string starts and where it ends. To clarify further, below I have temporarily changed line 7 so that it now puts asterisks rather than quotation marks before and after each key:

```
i   1▾ <script>
    2▾ function print_object(the_object) {
    3▾     document.write('{<br>');
    4▾     for(var i in the_object) {
    5          var key = i;
    6          var value = the_object[i];
    7          document.write('*' + key + '*');
    8          document.write(' : ');
    9          document.write(value);
    10         document.write('<br>');
    11     }
    12     document.write('}<br>');
    13 }
```

```
{
*maker* : Honda
*year* : 2018
}
```

Printing nested objects

The above printing function only works on simple objects. If we pass it an object that contains another object, the following happens:

```
i  1▾ <script>
   2▾ function print_object(the_object) {
   3▾     document.write('{<br>');
   4▾     for(var i in the_object) {
   5          var key = i;
   6          var value = the_object[i];
   7          document.write('"' + key + '"');
   8          document.write(' : ');
   9          document.write(value);
  10          document.write('<br>');
  11      }
  12      document.write('}<br>');
  13  }
  14
  15▾ var car = {
  16      "maker" : "Honda",
  17      "year": 2018,
  18▾     "model_details" : {
  19          "name" : "Accord",
  20          "length" : '192"',
  21          "width" : '73" W',
  22          "height" : '57" H',
  23      }
  24  }
  25  print_object(car);
  26  </script>
```

```
{
"maker" : Honda
"year" : 2018
"model_details" : [object Object]
}
```

As you can see, the **model_details** property is printed out as **[object Object]**. This is because on line 9 the **document.write(value)** statement forces JavaScript to interpret the nested object as a string. Since JavaScript is not designed to handle this, it simply tells us that we are trying to force an object to become a string.

In order to make **print_object** handle nested objects, we use a technique known as recursion:

```
 i   1▼ <script>
     2▼ function print_object(the_object) {
     3▼     document.write('{<br>');
     4▼     for(var i in the_object) {
     5          var key = i;
     6          var value = the_object[i];
     7          document.write('"' + key + '"');
     8          document.write(' : ');
     9▼         if(typeof value != 'object') {
    10              document.write(value);
    11          }
    12▼         else {
    13              print_object(value);
    14          }
    15          document.write('<br>');
    16      }
    17      document.write('}<br>');
    18  }
```

```
{
"maker" : Honda
"year" : 2018
"model_details" : {
"name" : Accord
"length" : 192"
"width" : 73" W
"height" : 57" H
}

}
```

On line 9 we use the new **typeof** operator, which is used to check the data type of a variable. The check **if(typeof value != 'object')** means "if the data type of the **value** variable is not the object data type". We are saying if the current property we are dealing with is not an object, then do the normal thing on line 10, which is to use **document.write()** to print out its contents. But if it *is* an object, meaning if we are dealing with a nested object, then instead the **else** part runs. In the **else** part we do something wonderful that programming allows us to do, which is to use a function inside itself. If we are printing a nested object, we simply call a new instance of the **print_object** function to print that nested object. This means that even if we had a dozen objects nested in one another, this function could handle them. Each time it sees a nested object, it passes control to a new version of the **print_object** function that deals specifically with the nested object.

When the loop inside **print_object()** function reaches the **model_details** property, the **else** part runs. The value variable that we pass into the second **print_object()** function on line 13 is actually an object, as if we had written:

```
else {
    print_object(
        {
            "name" : "Accord",
            "length" : '192"',
            "width" : '73" W',
            "height" : '57" H',
        }
    );
}
```

JavaScript starts a new separate instance of the **print_object()** function that deals solely with this nested object, not caring about the previous **print_object()** function that is also running. However, since JavaScript executes code line by line, the inner **print_object()** function has to finish like any other statement before JavaScript goes on with the loop in the outer **print_object()** function.

Recursion is relatively complicated and programmers rarely use it in their day-to-day work. But there are some situations that it is ideally suited for.

An object can also contain an array, and that array could in turn contain objects. Our function cannot handle such situations. Well, it can handle them, but it mistakenly thinks arrays are objects, as follows:

```
20 ▾ var car = {
21       "maker" : "Honda",
22       "year": 2018,
23 ▾     "model_details" : {
24           "name" : "Accord",
25           "length" : '192"',
26           "width" : '73" W',
27           "height" : '57" H',
28       },
29 ▾     "configurations" : [
30 ▾         {
31               'name': 'LX',
32               'msrp': '23570',
33           },
34 ▾         {
35               'name' : 'Sport CVT',
36               'msrp' : '25780',
37           },
38 ▾         {
39               'name' : 'Sport Manual',
40               'msr' : '25780'
41           }
42       ],
43  }
44  print_object(car);
45  </script>
46
```

```
{
"maker" : Honda
"year" : 2018
"model_details" : {
"name" : Accord
"length" : 192"
"width" : 73" W
"height" : 57" H
}

"configurations" : {
"0" : {
"name" : LX
"msrp" : 23570
}

"1" : {
"name" : Sport CVT
"msrp" : 25780
}
```

The reason it works is that **for** loops work on both arrays and objects. But as you can see in the preview area, the **configurations** property is printed with curly braces after it even though its value is an array.

Let us update it so that it can handle them. First we need a **print_array()** function for printing arrays:

```
19 ▾ function print_array(the_array) {
20 ▾     document.write('[<br>');
21 ▾     for(var i in the_array) {
22           var value = the_array[i];
23 ▾         if(Array.isArray(value)) {
24               print_array(value);
25           }
26 ▾         else if(typeof value === 'object') {
27               print_object(value);
28           }
29 ▾         else {
30               document.write(value + ',');
31           }
32       }
33       document.write(']<br>');
34  }
```

The principles used in this function are similar to those in **print_object()**. However we now have three checks inside the loop. We first use **Array.isArray()**, which is a special JavaScript function that checks if something is an array or not. In the **else if** part on line

26 we use the already-seen **typeof** operator to check if the **value** is an object. And if it is anything else we print it out normally.

We now have to update the **print_object()** function as well to recognize arrays. The original check was as follows:

```
 9 ▾        if(typeof value != 'object') {
10              document.write(value);
11          }
12 ▾        else {
13              print_object(value);
14          }
```

The **typeof** operator returns "object" for arrays as well, so it is useless for determining whether something is an array or an object. This is why we used **Array.isArray()** above to check if something is an array. We have to do the same here:

```
 9 ▾        if(Array.isArray(value)) {
10              print_array(value);
11          }
12 ▾        else if(typeof value === 'object') {
13              print_object(value);
14          }
15 ▾        else {
16              document.write(value);
17          }
```

We first have to check whether value is an array or not. If we put the **typeof value === 'object'** check first, that would stop our code from working properly, because **typeof value === 'object'** is true regardless of whether **value** is an array or an object. So first we have to check if it is an array. If it is not an array but it is an object according to **typeof**, it means it really is an object. Lastly we have an **else** statement for printing plain variables.

Below I have used the new code to print the cars object:

```
{
"maker" : Honda
"year" : 2018
"model_details" : {
"name" : Accord
"length" : 192"
"width" : 73" W
"height" : 57" H
}

"configurations" : [
{
"name" : LX
"msrp" : 23570
}
{
"name" : Sport CVT
"msrp" : 25780
}
{
"name" : Sport Manual
"msr" : 25780
}
]
```

As you can see, the **configurations** property is correctly recognized as an array, while the objects inside it are recognized and printed as objects.

Converting Arrays to Objects

In this section we will add functions (in addition to **print_object()** and **print_array()**) to turn arrays into an objects. Arrays are one-dimensional, while objects are two-dimensional. This gives us multiple options for converting arrays to objects:

```
39   var my_array = ['a', 'b', 'c'];
40 ▾ var my_first_object = {
41       'a' : '',
42       'b' : '',
43       'c' : '',
44   };
45 ▾ var my_second_object = {
46       0 : 'a',
47       1 : 'b',
48       2 : 'c',
49   };
50 ▾ var my_third_object = {
51       1 : 'a',
52       2 : 'b',
53       3 : 'c',
54   }
```

Above, on line 39 we have an array that contains three strings. Below that we have three ways of putting these strings into objects. In the first method we create an object whose keys are the same as the array elements, but whose values are empty strings. In the second method, we create an object whose keys are the same as the array index numbers, and whose values are the strings. In the method, we create an object whose keys start from 1 rather than zero, because the keys can be anything we want.

```
39 ▾ function array_to_object_1(my_array) {
40       var my_object = {};
41 ▾     for(var i in my_array) {
42           var the_element = my_array[i];
43           my_object[the_element] = '';
44       }
45       return my_object;
46   }
47
48   var my_array = ['a', 'b', 'c'];
49   print_object(array_to_object_1(my_array));
50   </script>
```

Above I have added a function to convert arrays to objects using the first method. Here is the result in the preview area:

```
{
"a" :
"b" :
"c" :
}
```

Below is a function to convert arrays to objects using the second method. The function is only slightly different from the previous one:

```
39 ▾ function array_to_object_1(my_array) {
40       var my_object = {};
41 ▾     for(var i in my_array) {
42           var the_element = my_array[i];
43           my_object[the_element] = '';
44       }
45       return my_object;
46   }
47
48 ▾ function array_to_object_2(my_array) {
49       var my_object = {};
50 ▾     for(var i in my_array) {
51           var the_element = my_array[i];
52           my_object[i] = the_element;
53       }
54       return my_object;
55   }
56
57   var my_array = ['a', 'b', 'c'];
58   print_object(array_to_object_2(my_array));
```

Here is the result:

```
{
"0" : a
"1" : b
"2" : c
}
```

Here is the third function:

```
57 ▾ function array_to_object_3(my_array) {
58           var my_object = {};
59 ▾     for(var i in my_array) {
60           var the_element = my_array[i];
61           var the_key = i + 1;
62           my_object[the_key] = the_element;
63       }
64       return my_object;
65   }
66
67   var my_array = ['a', 'b', 'c'];
68   print_object(array_to_object_3(my_array));
```

And here is the result:

```
{
"11" : b
"21" : c
"01" : a
}
```

Oops! We have a problem. On line 61, when we write **var the_key = i + 1**, JavaScript mistakenly thinks we are trying to concatenate two strings instead of adding two numbers. The result is that when i contains "1", JavaScript thinks **"1" + 1** equals **"11"**, similar to the way **"a" + 1** equals the string **"a1"**. To fix this error, we need a way to force JavaScript to interpret **i** as a number rather than as a string.

The simplest way to make JavaScript interpret a variable as a number is to multiply the variable by 1. Since multiplication only works on numbers, JavaScript is forced to see the variable as a number:

```
57 ▾ function array_to_object_3(my_array) {
58        var my_object = {};
59 ▾    for(var i in my_array) {
60          var the_element = my_array[i];
61          var the_key = (i * 1) + 1;
62          my_object[the_key] = the_element;
63      }
64      return my_object;
65  }
```

Above, on line 61 we multiply **i** by 1. This does not change the value of i but makes JavaScript see it as a number. The brackets are not necessary, but they help make it clear what we are doing. The function now works properly:

```
{
"1" : a
"2" : b
"3" : c
}
```

Calculating Word Frequencies

We will now go back to the Text Analyzer program to add a new function to it. This new function will calculate how many times each word occurs in the text. We already did something similar with students' first names. This time, now that we have access to objects, we can do things much more efficiently. First, I move the text to the top of the code since it is taking up a lot of screen space. On line 15 I put the **text** variable inside **text_analyzer.current_word** to keep things just as before:

```
i  1 ▾ <script>
   2    var text =
   3        'And this is Dorlcote Mill. I must '
   4        + 'stand a minute or two here on the bridge '
   5        + 'and look at it, though the clouds are '
   6        + 'threatening, and it is far on in the afternoon. '
   7        + 'Even in this leafless time of departing February '
   8        + 'it is pleasant to look at,-perhaps the chill, '
   9        + 'damp season adds a charm to the trimly kept, '
  10        + 'comfortable dwelling-house, as old as the elms '
  11        + 'and chestnuts that shelter it from the '
  12        + 'northern blast. ';
  13
  14 ▾ var text_analyzer = {
  15        current_text : text,
  16 ▾      get_words_array : function() {
```

Below we add the new **get_word_frequencies()** function on lines 51-69:

```
 51 ▾      get_word_frequencies : function() {
 52            var words_array = this.get_words_array();
 53            var word_frequencies = {};
 54 ▾          for(var i in words_array) {
 55                var current_word = words_array[i];
 56 ▾              if(! (current_word in word_frequencies)) {
 57                    word_frequencies[current_word] = 1;
 58                }
 59 ▾              else {
 60                    var previous_frequency =
 61                        word_frequencies[current_word];
 62                    var new_frequency = previous_frequency
 63                        + 1;
 64                    word_frequencies[current_word] =
 65                        new_frequency;
 66                }
 67            }
 68            return word_frequencies;
 69        },
 70 };
 71
 72 var frequencies = text_analyzer.get_word_frequencies();
 73 ▾ for(var i in frequencies) {
 74        document.write(i + ': ' + frequencies[i] + '<br>');
 75 }
 76 </script>
 77
 78
 79
```

And: 1
this: 2
is: 3
Dorlcote: 1
Mill.: 1
I: 1
must: 1
stand: 1
a: 2
minute: 1
or: 1
two: 1
here: 1
on: 2
the: 7
bridge: 1
and: 3
look: 2
at: 1
it.: 1
though: 1
clouds: 1

The **get_word_frequencies()** function goes over all of the words in the text one by one and uses the object **word_frequencies** to keep track of how many times each word is seen in the loop. On line 56 we use something we have not seen before to check whether the **word_frequencies** object has a particular property or not. When the **current_word** variable contains the word "And", the check **if(! (current_word in word_frequencies))** is interpreted by JavaScript as **if(! ("And" in**

word_frequencies)), which checks whether the **word_frequencies** object has a property named **And** or not. Since the condition starts with an exclamation mark, that makes the whole condition negative, meaning the check is if *not* **And** exists in **word_frequencies**. We write it this way because we want the code below it to create the property if it does not exist, so we are saying *if it does not exist, then do this.*

If the property does not exist, then we create it using **word_frequencies[current_word] = 1** on line 57. This means that when **current_word** is "And", **word_frequencies["And"]** is created and set to 1 in one statement, as the following illustration shows:

```
if(! ("And" in word_frequencies)) {
    word_frequencies["And"] = 1;
}
```

As the loop goes on, the **word_frequencies** object is gradually filled up. Each element in the **words_array** is turned into a property of the **word_frequencies** object. They keys are all from the array, while all the values are 1. Here is a simple illustration of what we are creating with this loop:

```
var my_array = ["a", "b", "c"];
var my_object = {
    "a" : 1,
    "b" : 1,
    "c" : 1
}
```

However, if we see a word that we have already seen before, then the check on line 56 fails because **word_frequencies** will contain a key that is the same as that word, so that the **else** part of our code runs:

```
56 ▾    if(! (current_word in word_frequencies)) {
57          word_frequencies[current_word] = 1;
58      }
59 ▾    else {
60          var previous_frequency =
61              word_frequencies[current_word];
62          var new_frequency = previous_frequency
63              + 1;
64          word_frequencies[current_word] =
65              new_frequency;
66      }
```

If, for example, **word_frequencies["is"]** has already been seen once in the past, if we see it again, in the **else** part we first get the number of times it has been seen in the past using the statement **previous_frequency = word_frequencies[current_word]** on lines 60-61. We then add 1 to this number. Then we update **word_frequencies["is"]** so that it contains the new number. Below is a simple illustration of what is going on. The array **my_array** contains the string "a" three times, but all three "go into" the same key on **my_object**, while the value is increased to 3 to reflect how many times "a" is in **my_array**:

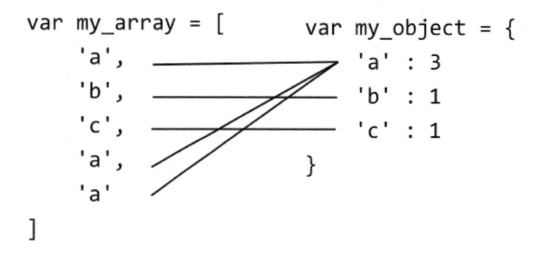

At this point we have finished explaining how the **get_word_frequencies()** function works. Below I use the **print_object()** function to print out the object returned by the function:

```
109   var frequencies = text_analyzer.get_word_frequencies();
110   print_object(frequencies);
111   </script>
```

Here is the result (partially shown due to being too long):

```
{
"And" : 1
"this" : 2
"is" : 3
"Dorlcote" : 1
"Mill." : 1
"I" : 1
"must" : 1
"stand" : 1
"a" : 2
"minute" : 1
"or" : 1
"two" : 1
"here" : 1
"on" : 2
"the" : 7
"bridge" : 1
"and" : 3
"look" : 2
"at" : 1
```

We can also use **get_word_frequencies()** to check the number of times one particular word occurs rather than printing out all of the results, as follows:

```
109    var frequencies = text_analyzer.get_word_frequencies();
110    document.write(frequencies['on']);
```

Here is the result:

2

We can shorten the above two lines into one line:

```
109    document.write(text_analyzer.get_word_frequencies()['on']);
```

At this point we have covered the basics of objects. If you find objects confusing, feel free to forget about them for now and review them days or weeks later. You can create any program you can imagine without using objects. But once you are used to them, you will find many uses for them.

10. Regular Expressions

Regular expressions enable us to use patterns to do search and replace within a piece of text. You may have used "wildcards" in programs like Microsoft Word. Below is an example in which we put the wildcard **c?t** in Word's Find and Replace dialog:

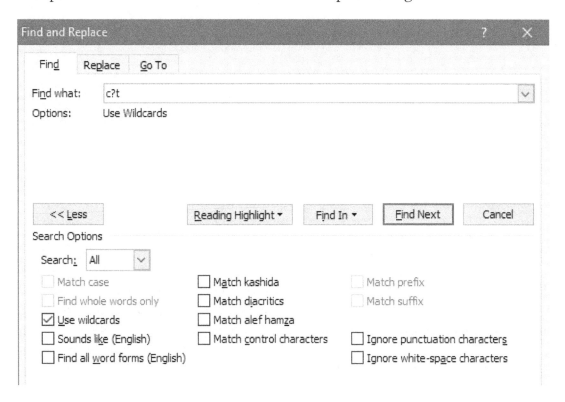

In Word, doing a wildcard search for **c?t** finds any 3-character string that starts with a c and ends with "t", such as "cat" and "cot".

In JavaScript, regular expressions help us achieve the same kind of thing. Below we use a regular expression to check whether the string variable **text** contains the string "is a":

```
 1 ▾ <script>
 2    var text = 'It is a good day';
 3
 4    var my_regular_expression = /is a/;
 5    document.write(my_regular_expression.test(text));
 6    </script>
```
true

The regular expression is on line 4. It starts with a forward slash and ends with a forward slash. Regular expressions are not strings, arrays, plain objects or any other data type. They are their own independent thing. On line 5, we use the **test()** function (which only works on regular expressions) to test whether the text variable satisfies the regular expression or not. The result is a boolean "true" as seen in the preview area, meaning that the text variable does indeed satisfy the **/is a/** regular expression (since it contains "is a").

Below we change the regular expression to test whether the string contains "it" or not:

```
 1 ▾ <script>
 2    var text = 'It is a good day';
 3
 4    var my_regular_expression = /it/;
 5    document.write(my_regular_expression.test(text));
 6    </script>
```
false

The result is false because the variable **text** contains "It", not "it". We can make our regular expression case-insensitive so that it will match both uppercase and lowercase characters as follows:

```
 1 ▾ <script>
 2    var text = 'It is a good day';
 3
 4    var my_regular_expression = /it/i;
 5    document.write(my_regular_expression.test(text));
 6    </script>
```
true

Above, I have added an **i** after the regular expression's ending slash on line 4. This is called a "modifier", it modifies how the regular expression works. The **i** stands for insensitive, making the regular expression insensitive to the difference between upper and lower case characters so that it matches both.

Since the **test()** function returns a boolean **true** or **false**, we can use it in if statements as follows:

```
i  1▾ <script>
   2   var text = 'It is a good day';
   3
   4   var my_regular_expression = /day/i;
   5▾  if(my_regular_expression.test(text)) {
   6       document.write('The string has '
   7       + '"day" in it!');
   8   }
   9   </script>
```

The string has "day" in it!

We can also use a regular expression directly without putting it in a variable:

```
i  1▾ <script>
   2   var text = 'It is a good day';
   3
   4▾  if(/day/i.test(text)) {
   5       document.write('The string has '
   6       + '"day" in it!');
   7   }
   8   </script>
```

The string has "day" in it!

Besides the **test()** function, we also have the more interesting **match()** function. This function is actually a string function, meaning that it has to be called on strings rather than regular expressions, so that using this function is reverse of the way we used the test() function.

```
i  1▾ <script>
   2   var text = 'It is a good day';
   3
   4   var my_regular_expression = /good/;
   5   var matches = text.match(my_regular_expression);
   6   document.write(matches.toString());
   7   </script>
```

good

The **text.match()** function returns an array that contains all the strings matched by the regular expression we give to it. Above, we search for "good", and unsurprisingly, the matches array contains "good" as its only element when we print it out.

Below I update the text variable so that it now contains another passage from *The Mill on the Floss*. I have made the whole passage fit on one line in the code in order to save space. On line 3 I have printed out the **text** variable so that you can see part of the string in the preview area.

```
i  1▾ <script>
   2   var text = 'The rush of the water and the booming
   3   document.write(text);
   4   var my_regular_expression = /good/;
   5   var matches = text.match(my_regular_expression);
   6   document.write(matches.toString());
   7   </script>
   8
   9
  10
  11
  12
  13
  14
  15
  16
  17
  18
  19
  20
```

The rush of the water and the booming of the mill bring a dreamy deafness, which seems to heighten the peacefulness of the scene. They are like a great curtain of sound, shutting one out from the world beyond. And now there is the thunder of the huge covered wagon coming home with sacks of grain. That honest wagoner is thinking of his dinner, getting sadly dry in the oven at this late hour; but he will not touch it till he has fed his horses,—the strong, submissive,

I now remove the **document.write()** statement on line 3. The code shown earlier actually causes an error in JavaScript when we run it. When looking at the console we see the following:

```
▶Uncaught TypeError: Cannot read property 'toString' of null
    at <anonymous>:6:23
```

This cryptic error message is telling us we have used the **toString()** function on line 6 on something that is **null**. What it actually means is that the **matches** array is not actually an array, it is **null**. This is because the new string inside **text** does not contain the word "good" that we are searching for. The **match()** function on line 5 returns **null**. This means that the **matches** variable contains **null**, so that using **toString()** on it leads to an error and breaks our code, since **toString()** is not designed to be used on variables that contain **null**. To avoid this error, we have to check whether the **matches** array is null or not before we try to print it out:

```
i  1▾ <script>
   2   var text = 'The rush of the water and the booming
   3
   4   var my_regular_expression = /good/;
   5   var matches = text.match(my_regular_expression);
   6▾  if(matches === null) {
   7       document.write('No matches found!');
   8   }
   9▾  else {
  10       document.write(matches.toString())
  11   }
  12   </script>
```

No matches found!

Above, we check if **matches** is **null** on line 6. If so, we print out a helpful message. If it is not **null**, then we use **toString()** to print out its contents on line 10.

Below, we update the regular expression to search for " the " (a space followed by "the" followed by a space):

```
i   1 ▾ <script>
    2   var text = 'The rush of the water and the booming       the
    3
    4   var my_regular_expression = / the /;
    5   var matches = text.match(my_regular_expression);
    6 ▾ if(matches === null) {
    7       document.write('No matches found!');
    8   }
    9 ▾ else {
   10       document.write(matches.toString())
   11   }
   12 </script>
```

In the preview area only one " the " gets printed out even though the **text** variable obviously contains multiple occurrences of the word "the". This is caused by the fact that JavaScript regular expressions by default stop searching once they find a single match. In order to find all occurrences of a word, we have to use the **g** modifier (which stands for "global"), as follows:

```
i   1 ▾ <script>
    2   var text = 'The rush of the water and the booming    the , the , the , the , the , the , the ,
    3                                                         the , the , the , the , the , the , the ,
    4   var my_regular_expression = / the /g;                 the , the , the , the , the , the , the ,
    5   var matches = text.match(my_regular_expression);      the , the
    6 ▾ if(matches === null) {
    7       document.write('No matches found!');
    8   }
    9 ▾ else {
   10       document.write(matches.toString())
   11   }
   12 </script>
```

Now all occurrences of " the " are printed out. That is not very useful at the moment. One use of this code however would be to find out how many times the string we are searching for occurs in the text, as follows:

```
 i   1 ▾ <script>
     2     var text = 'The rush of the water and the booming
     3
     4     var my_regular_expression = / the /g;
     5     var matches = text.match(my_regular_expression);
     6 ▾ if(matches === null) {
     7         document.write('No matches found!');
     8     }
     9 ▾ else {
    10         document.write(matches.length)
    11     }
    12   </script>
```
23

Above, I have changed line 10 to print out the length of the matches array, which equals 23, meaning that " the " occurs 23 times inside the **text** variable.

We can now move on to the more interesting part of regular expression, wildcards. The following regular expression matches all 3-character-long strings starting with an "a":

```
 1 ▾ <script>
 2     var text = 'The rush of the water and the booming
 3
 4     var my_regular_expression = /a../g;
 5     var matches = text.match(my_regular_expression);
 6 ▾ if(matches === null) {
 7         document.write('No matches found!');
 8     }
 9 ▾ else {
10         document.write(matches.toString())
11     }
12   </script>
```

ate,and,a d,amy,afn,ace,are,a g,at ,ain,ago,ack,ain,at ,ago,adl,at ,ate,as ,ast,anc,are,ach,at ,at ,ack,at ,at ,awf,ann,as ,at ,ard,all,aus,are,ar ,at ,and,agg,at ,asp,art,at ,ati,avy,ar,,at ,aun,ar ,ard,arn,and,arn,age,are,and,aga,at ,a s,ace,and,arc,ago,app,ars,at

The regular expression **/a../g** means "a string starting with a, followed by any character, followed by any character". Inside regular expressions dots stand for "any character". The preview area shows us a large number of matches. The results are messy because the regular expression matches inside words and between words. The first match is "ate", which is from the word "water". JavaScript does not care that this match is in the middle of a word since we have not told it to care. There is also the match "a g" (a followed by a space followed by a g) which is from the string "a great". The dot wildcard matches spaces too, so this is a perfectly good match.

We can improve the results we get by updating the regular expression to have a space before and after it:

```
i  1 ▾ <script>
   2    var text = 'The rush of the water and the booming
   3
   4    var my_regular_expression = / a.. /g;
   5    var matches = text.match(my_regular_expression);
   6 ▾  if(matches === null) {
   7        document.write('No matches found!');
   8    }
   9 ▾  else {
  10        document.write(matches.toString())
  11    }
  12    </script>
```

and , are , are , all , are , and , are ,
and , and

Above, I have changed **/a../g** to **/ a.. /g**. The meaning of the new regular expression is "a space, followed by an a, followed by any character, followed by any character, followed by a space". This

The next wildcard we will look at is the question mark wildcard. This wildcard makes the pattern that comes before it optional.

```
 1 ▾ <script>
 2    var text = 'The rush of the water and the booming
 3
 4    var my_regular_expression = / a?.. /g;
 5    var matches = text.match(my_regular_expression);
 6 ▾  if(matches === null) {
 7        document.write('No matches found!');
 8    }
 9 ▾  else {
10        document.write(matches.toString())
11    }
12    </script>
```

of , and , of , to , of , are , of , is , of
, of , is , of , in , at , he , it , he , are ,
at , he , at , in , as , up , all , are , at ,
to , at , of , at , of , to , of , and , are ,
and , go , at , and , of , at

Above I have added a question mark right after the "a" in the regular expression on line 4. The result is that we now have many more matches. The regular expression **/ a?.. /g** means: "(a space)('a' or nothing)(any character)(any character)(a space)". The question mark with the "a" makes the "a" optional, so that the regular expression will match any string that matches the rest of the pattern whether or not the "a" is present at that place. The result is that "of" is the first match we get.

Below I move the question mark behind the last dot:

```
1 ▾ <script>
2   var text = 'The rush of the water and the booming
3
4   var my_regular_expression = / a..? /g;
5   var matches = text.match(my_regular_expression);
6 ▾ if(matches === null) {
7       document.write('No matches found!');
8   }
9 ▾ else {
10      document.write(matches.toString())
11  }
12  </script>
```

and , are , at , are , at , at , as , all , are , at , at , at , and , are , and , at , and , at

The new regular expression means: "(a space)(an 'a')(any character)(any character or nothing)(a space)". The result is that it matches all two and three-character-long strings that start with a.

Regular expressions like a programming language within a programming language. They have their own syntax and logic, for this reason it will take learners a long time to familiarize themselves with them and master them. Like everything else in programming, reading and writing code is the best way to learn how to use regular expressions.

Replacing strings

The **replace()** function allows us to use patterns to replace one part of a string with something else. This function takes two arguments. The first argument is a pattern. The second argument is the string we want to replace the pattern with:

```
i  1 ▾ <script>
   2   var text = 'The rush of the water and the
   3   text = text.replace(/r/, 'b');
   4   document.write(text);
   5   </script>
   6
   7
```

The bush of the water and the booming of the mill bring a dreamy deafness, which seems to heighten the peacefulness of the scene.

Above, we have given the regular expression **/r/** as the first argument to **replace()**. The second argument is the string 'b'. This tells JavaScript to replace the string that matches **/r/** with the string "b". The result is that the word rush is now "bush" in the preview area. Below I add the **g** modifier to the regular expression, so that it now replaces *all* of the matches of the pattern not just the first one:

```
i  1 ▾ <script>
   2    var text = 'The rush of the water and the
   3    text = text.replace(/r/g, 'b');
   4    document.write(text);
   5    </script>
   6
   7
```

> The bush of the wateb and
> the booming of the mill
> bbing a dbeamy deafness,
> which seems to heighten the
> peacefulness of the scene.

Above, you can see that the word "water" has become "wateb" in the preview area, since are now replacing all r's with b's.

Now onto a useful example What if your boss gave you a list of 10,000 names and asked you to turn every middle name to an initial (for example Henry Newton Smith would become Henry N. Smith)? We can accomplish this in a few relatively simple lines. In our example, we will use the names of three American economists to simply the example:

```
i  1 ▾ <script>
   2 ▾ var american_economists = [
   3            'Henry Charles Carey',
   4            'Erasmus Peshine Smith',
   5            'George Ernest Barnett',
   6        ];
   7
   8    var shortened_names = [];
   9
  10 ▾ for(var i in american_economists) {
  11        var economist
  12            = american_economists[i];
  13        var shortened =
  14            economist.replace(/ ([A-Z])[a-z]+ /,
  15            ' $1. ');
  16        shortened_names.push(shortened);
  17    }
  18
  19    document.write(shortened_names.join('<br>'));
  20    </script>
```

> Henry C. Carey
> Erasmus P. Smith
> George E. Barnett

The code should be self-explanatory except for lines 14 and 15. An illustration is perhaps the best way to explain the regular expression on line 14:

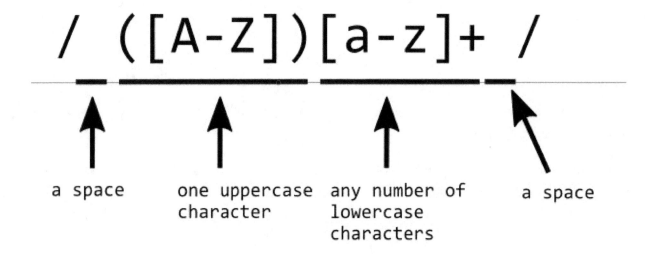

We have a number of new concepts in this regular expression. The first one is the stuff in the square brackets, such as **[A-Z]**. This is known as a character class and means "any character between uppercase A and uppercase Z". We also have another character class **[a-z]** which means "any character between lowercase a and lowercase z". The first character class is inside round brackets **([A-Z])**. Inside regular expressions brackets have a very special meaning and the stuff inside them is known as a "capturing group". They tell JavaScript to store the stuff in the brackets in a variable that we can later refer to using a dollar sign and a number (that is what the **$1** on line 15 does).

The other new thing is the plus sign after the second character class. This sign means "one or more of the preceding pattern". In other words, **[a-z]+** means "one or more lowercase characters.

The regular expression as a whole matches middle names, since middle names have a space before them, start with an uppercase character and have any number of lowercase characters after that and have a space after them.

The second argument of the **replace()** function is **' $1. '**. This means "a space, followed by whatever was matched by the capturing group, followed by a space. If the regular expression on line 14 had matched " Charles ", since the capturing group on line 14 only captures the first character of the name, all of the string " Charles" is replaced by " C. ".

All of lines 14 and 15 can be interpreted as "find a middle name, save the first character of the middle name in a variable named **$1**, then replace all of the middle name with the value inside this variable, followed by a dot."

Comments

In programming, comments are pieces of text inside our code that do nothing. They are just there for the benefit of programmers, to help them understand the code better. Below I have added a comment on line 13:

```
10 ▾ for(var i in american_economists) {
11       var economist
12           = american_economists[i];
13       var shortened = // the middle initial
14           economist.replace(/ ([A-Z])[a-z]+ /,
15           ' $1. ');
16       shortened_names.push(shortened);
17   }
```

The comment on line 13 starts with a double forward slash. This tells JavaScript this is a comment. Anything after the double slashes will be ignored by JavaScript, but programmers reading the code will have an easier time understanding what the code does, since it will not be obvious even to an experienced programmer what the regular expression does unless they wait for a few seconds to decipher it. But if they see the comment, they can instantly realize that it is trying to get the middle initial of the name.

The above type of comment is known as a single line comment. We also have mutli-line comments that allow us to write whole paragraphs of text as a comment:

```
 9 ▾ /*
10   This loop goes through the full names
11   and initializes the middle names
12   while leaving the first and last names
13   intact.
14   */
15 ▾ for(var i in american_economists) {
16       var economist
17           = american_economists[i];
18       var shortened = // the middle initial
19           economist.replace(/ ([A-Z])[a-z]+ /,
20           ' $1. ');
21       shortened_names.push(shortened);
22   }
```

A multi-line comment starts with a slash followed by an asterisk (line 9) and ends with an asterisk followed by a slash (line 14).

Instead of using a multi-line comment we can use multiple single line comments as follows:

```
10   // This loop goes through the full names
11   // and initializes the middle names
12   // while leaving the first and last names
13   // intact.
14 ▾ for(var i in american_economists) {
15       var economist
16           = american_economists[i];
17       var shortened = // the middle initial
18           economist.replace(/ ([A-Z])[a-z]+ /,
19           ' $1. ');
20       shortened_names.push(shortened);
21   }
```

It is always best to write your code to be self-explanatory so that it will not require comments. By giving your variables and functions easy-to-understand names, the code will be easy to understand. Regular expressions, however, are an exception. It is almost always a good idea to write a comment explaining what the regular expression does, otherwise if you are reading your own code months later you may have no idea what the regular expression is meant to do and may waste many precious minutes deciphering its purpose.

Counting Names

In this section we will examine a real-world file and run some JavaScript on it. The file we will use is the entire text of the novel *The Mill on the Floss* by George Eliot, freely available at the Project Gutenberg website. Below is a screenshot of the novel as opened on my computer in the Chromium web browser:

In order to use JavaScript on this document we have to open the console (you can right click on an empty area in the document click "Inspect" or something similar, as explained in chapter 2). With the console open, I click the "Console" tab, which currently shows up as a blank area:

The first thing to do is to put the entire text of the novel inside a single variable. To do so we use the statement shown below:

The property **document.documentElement.innerText** is a special JavaScript variable that retrieves all of the text in the document. Once we press Enter (or similar), the console runs the code and prints out "undefined":

The "undefined" in this case simply means our statement returned nothing. This is not a bad thing. Since we putting one variable inside another, there is nothing to print out yet.

The console works on a line-by-line basis. You write one statement, press Enter, then go to onto the next statement. You can also write multiple statements by pressing Shift+Enter to create a new line.

Below, I use the **match()** function to attempt to find the full names of all the characters mentioned in the novel:

```
> text.match(/[A-Z][a-z]+ [A-Z][a-z]+/g);
  (964) ["The Project", "The Mill", "George Eliot", "United States", "Project Gutenberg", "United States"
  , "The Mill", "George Eliot", "Posting Date", "Release Date", "First Posted", "Curtis Weyant", "David M
  addock", "The Mill", "George Eliot", "Outside Dorlcote", "Dorlcote Mill", "Declares His", "Riley Gives"
  , "His Advice", "Tom Is", "Tom Comes", "The Aunts", "Uncles Are", "Tulliver Shows", "His Weaker", "To G
  arum", "Maggie Behaves", "Worse Than", "She Expected", "Maggie Tries", "Her Shadow", "Tulliver Further"
  , "First Half", "The Christmas", "The New", "The Young", "Second Visit", "The Golden", "Gates Are", "Th
  e Downfall", "What Had", "Household Gods", "The Family", "Vanishing Gleam", "Tom Applies", "His Knife",
  ▶ "Popular Prejudice", "Hen Takes", "An Item", "Family Register", "The Valley", "Protestantism Unknown",
    "The Torn", "Nest Is", "Red Deeps", "Aunt Glegg", "The Wavering", "Another Love", "The Cloven", "The H
  ard", "Won Triumph", "The Great", "First Impressions", "Confidential Moments", "Showing That", "Tom Had
  ", "Philip Re", "New Light", "The Spell", "Seems Broken", "Family Party", "Borne Along", "The Final", "
  The Return", "Passes Judgment", "Showing That", "Old Acquaintances", "Are Capable", "Surprising Us", "T
  he Last", "Outside Dorlcote", "Dorlcote Mill", "Dorlcote Mill", "Dorlcote Mill", "Declares His", "Lawye
  r Wakem", "John Gibbs", "As Mrs", "If Mr", "Exit Maggie", "Riley Gives", "His Advice", "Old Harry", "Ol
  d Harry", "Even Hotspur", "Daniel Defoe", "Jeremy Taylor", "Holy Living", "But Stelling", …]
```

The regular expression I use is **/[A-Z][a-z]+ [A-Z][a-z]+/g**, which means "an uppercase word followed by a space followed by an uppercase word". When we run the statement, the console immediately prints out the result. The number 964 at the beginning tells us how many elements are in the returned array, meaning that our regular expression had 964 matches.

The console does not show us the fully array of matches because it is so large. But if we click on it, it will expand it as follows, showing us the index values:

```
▶ [0 … 99]
▶ [100 … 199]
▶ [200 … 299]
▶ [300 … 399]
▶ [400 … 499]
▶ [500 … 599]
▶ [600 … 699]
▶ [700 … 799]
▶ [800 … 899]
▶ [900 … 963]
  length: 964
▶ __proto__: Array(0)
```

Clicking on one of these number ranges further expands them:

```
▼ [800 … 899]
    800: "If Maggie"
    801: "Miss Tulliver"
    802: "Miss Tulliver"
    803: "Miss Tulliver"
    804: "When Maggie"
    805: "Showing That"
    806: "Old Acquaintances"
    807: "Are Capable"
    808: "Surprising Us"
    809: "When Maggie"
    810: "Then Mrs"
    811: "While Mrs"
    812: "But Tom"
```

Many of the values in the array are repetitions. We can fix that by creating a function that filters out all repeated values from an array. Below I define a new function, **get_unique_only()** right inside the console. The function is on multiple lines. As I mentioned earlier, to write a new line without the console running the code, you have to use Shift+Enter. Pressing Enter alone will make the console try to execute the incomplete code.

```
> function get_unique_only(my_array) {
      var my_set = new Set(my_array);
      var my_unique_array = Array.from(my_set);
      return my_unique_array;
  }
```

The function uses a clever trick to get all the unique values from an array. It first converts the array into a set (a set is a special data type in JavaScript inspired by mathematical sets, and it can only contain unique values) using **var my_set = new Set(my_array)**. It then converts the set back to an array using **Array.from(my_set)**. And that is all. This conversion back-and-forth conversion causes all duplicate values to wither away.

After writing out the function, I press Enter to make JavaScript run the code. The word "undefined" is printed out again, because I have only *defined* a function, I have not used it yet, so there is no return value. But the function remains there behind the scenes to be used later on.

```
> function get_unique_only(my_array) {
      var my_set = new Set(my_array);
      var my_unique_array = Array.from(my_set);
      return my_unique_array;
  }
< undefined
>
```

If you remember, earlier when I ran the **text.match(/[A-Z][a-z]+ [A-Z][a-z]+/g);** function I did not put the result inside a variable. Even though the console printed out the resulting array, the array is no longer available to me. I will run the code again but this time I will put the array inside its own variable:

```
> var array_full_of_duplicates = text.match(/[A-Z][a-z]+ [A-Z][a-z]+/g);
< undefined
```

Next I will declare a new array build using the new **get_unique_only()** function:

```
> var unique_array = get_unique_only(array_full_of_duplicates);
< undefined
```

And now, to actually show the result, we write the new array's name in the console then press Enter:

```
> unique_array
< (379) ["The Project", "The Mill", "George Eliot", "United States", "Project Gutenberg", "Posting Date",
  "Release Date", "First Posted", "Curtis Weyant", "David Maddock", "Outside Dorlcote", "Dorlcote Mill",
  "Declares His", "Riley Gives", "His Advice", "Tom Is", "Tom Comes", "The Aunts", "Uncles Are", "Tulliv
  er Shows", "His Weaker", "To Garum", "Maggie Behaves", "Worse Than", "She Expected", "Maggie Tries", "H
  er Shadow", "Tulliver Further", "First Half", "The Christmas", "The New", "The Young", "Second Visit",
  "The Golden", "Gates Are", "The Downfall", "What Had", "Household Gods", "The Family", "Vanishing Gleam
  ", "Tom Applies", "His Knife", "Popular Prejudice", "Hen Takes", "An Item", "Family Register", "The Val
▶ ley", "Protestantism Unknown", "The Torn", "Nest Is", "Red Deeps", "Aunt Glegg", "The Wavering", "Anoth
  er Love", "The Cloven", "The Hard", "Won Triumph", "The Great", "First Impressions", "Confidential Mome
  nts", "Showing That", "Tom Had", "Philip Re", "New Light", "The Spell", "Seems Broken", "Family Party",
  "Borne Along", "The Final", "The Return", "Passes Judgment", "Old Acquaintances", "Are Capable", "Surp
  rising Us", "The Last", "Lawyer Wakem", "John Gibbs", "As Mrs", "If Mr", "Exit Maggie", "Old Harry", "E
  ven Hotspur", "Daniel Defoe", "Jeremy Taylor", "Holy Living", "But Stelling", "Ask Mr", "Walter Stellin
  g", "Mudport Free", "De Senectute", "Louisa Timpson", "Thus Mr", "Animated Nature", "Master Tom", "Prod
  igal Son", "Sir Charles", "Round Pool", "Thus Maggie", "Tom Tulliver", "Great Ash", …]
```

Let's now check how many times the name of the heroine is used throughout the novel:

```
> text.match(/Maggie/g);
< (1402) ["Maggie", "Maggie", "Maggie", "Maggie", "Maggie", "Maggie", "Maggie", "Maggie", "Maggie", "Magg
  ie", "Maggie", "Maggie", "Maggie", "Maggie", "Maggie", "Maggie", "Maggie", "Maggie", "Maggie", "Maggie"
  , "Maggie", "Maggie", "Maggie", "Maggie", "Maggie", "Maggie", "Maggie", "Maggie", "Maggie", "Maggie", "
  Maggie", "Maggie", "Maggie", "Maggie", "Maggie", "Maggie", "Maggie", "Maggie", "Maggie", "Maggie", "Mag
▶ gie", "Maggie", "Maggie", "Maggie", "Maggie", "Maggie", "Maggie", "Maggie", "Maggie", "Maggie", "Maggie
  ", "Maggie", "Maggie", "Maggie", "Maggie", "Maggie", "Maggie", "Maggie", "Maggie", "Maggie", "Maggie",
  "Maggie", "Maggie", "Maggie", "Maggie", "Maggie", "Maggie", "Maggie", "Maggie", "Maggie", "Maggie", "Ma
  ggie", "Maggie", "Maggie", "Maggie", "Maggie", "Maggie", "Maggie", "Maggie", "Maggie", "Maggie", "Maggi
  e", "Maggie", "Maggie", "Maggie", "Maggie", "Maggie", "Maggie", "Maggie", "Maggie", "Maggie", "Maggie",
  "Maggie", "Maggie", "Maggie", "Maggie", "Maggie", "Maggie", "Maggie", "Maggie", …]
```

Apparently it is 1402 times. Since there is no point in seeing all those repeated Maggies printed out, we can simply get the length of the array:

```
> text.match(/Maggie/g).length;
< 1402
```

Let's now get the total number of words in the novel:

```
text.match(/ [A-Za-z]+ /g);

(92332) [" Project ", " EBook ", " The ", " on ", " by ", " eBook ", " for ", " use
    ", " anyone ", " in ", " United ", " and ", " parts ", " the ", " at ", " cost ",
    " with ", " no ", " You ", " copy ", " give ", " away ", " it ", " the ", " Project
    ", " License ", " with ", " eBook ", " online ", " If ", " are ", " located ", " t
    he ", " check ", " laws ", " the ", " where ", " are ", " before ", " this ", " The
    ", " on ", " George ", " September ", " January ", " set ", " START ", " THIS ", "
  ▶ GUTENBERG ", " THE ", " ON ", " FLOSS ", " by ", " Weyant ", " David ", " Mill ",
    " the ", " of ", " Boy ", " Dorlcote ", " of ", " Declares ", " Resolution ", " Ril
    ey ", " His ", " Concerning ", " School ", " Is ", " Comes ", " Aunts ", " Uncles "
    , " the ", " and ", " Tulliver ", " His ", " Garum ", " Behaves ", " Than ", " Trie
    s ", " Run ", " from ", " and ", " Glegg ", " Tulliver ", " Entangles ", " Skein ",
    " Christmas ", " New ", " Young ", " Second ", " Golden ", " Are ", " The ", " Had
    ", " at ", " or ", " Family ", " Vanishing ", " Applies ", " Knife ", …]
```

The result of 92332 is not perfect, but something of an approximation. The regular expression this time uses **[A-Za-z]+**, which means "one or more uppercase or lowercase characters". This means it will match "START", "anyone", "Garum", and any other mix of uppercase and lowercase characters.

Below I use the earlier **get_unique_only()** function to the number of unique words in the novel:

```
get_unique_only(text.match(/ [A-Za-z]+ /g));

(7731) [" Project ", " EBook ", " The ", " on ", " by ", " eBook ", " for ", " use
    ", " anyone ", " in ", " United ", " and ", " parts ", " the ", " at ", " cost ", "
    with ", " no ", " You ", " copy ", " give ", " away ", " it ", " License ", " onli
    ne ", " If ", " are ", " located ", " check ", " laws ", " where ", " before ", " t
    his ", " George ", " September ", " January ", " set ", " START ", " THIS ", " GUTE
    NBERG ", " THE ", " ON ", " FLOSS ", " Weyant ", " David ", " Mill ", " of ", " Boy
  ▶ ", " Dorlcote ", " Declares ", " Resolution ", " Riley ", " His ", " Concerning ",
    " School ", " Is ", " Comes ", " Aunts ", " Uncles ", " Tulliver ", " Garum ", " B
    ehaves ", " Than ", " Tries ", " Run ", " from ", " Glegg ", " Entangles ", " Skein
    ", " Christmas ", " New ", " Young ", " Second ", " Golden ", " Are ", " Had ", "
    or ", " Family ", " Vanishing ", " Applies ", " Knife ", " to ", " Prejudice ", "
    a ", " Takes ", " Item ", " Variation ", " Protestantism ", " Torn ", " Voice ", "
    Wheat ", " Wavering ", " Cloven ", " Day ", " Duet ", " That ", " Spell ", " Along
    ", " Return ", " Passes ", …]
```

If we want to show the number only, we can again use the **length** property at the end of the statement:

```
> get_unique_only(text.match(/ [A-Za-z]+ /g)).length;
← 7731
```

At this point you have been exposed to a few regular expressions to help you see what they are. We only scratched the surface of what regular expressions can do as it is not within the scope of this book to cover them comprehensively.

11. Sorting and Filtering

In this chapter we will discuss two common operations in programming; sorting and filtering.

The **sort()** function sorts an array from the lowest value to the highest value:

```
1 ▼ <script>
2     var numbers = [1, 5, 3, 4, 2];
3     var sorted_numbers = numbers.sort();
4     document.write(sorted_numbers.join('<br>'));
5   </script>
6
7
```
```
1
2
3
4
5
```

On line 2 we have an array that contains a mix of numbers. On line 3 we use **numbers.sort()** to sort the numbers. The result, as seen in the preview area, is that the numbers are now sorted from smallest to largest.

Sorting of numbers will not work properly if the numbers are strings, as follows:

```
1 ▼ <script>
2     var numbers = ["1", "11", "2", "25"];
3     var sorted_numbers = numbers.sort();
4     document.write(sorted_numbers.join('<br>'));
5   </script>
6
```
```
1
11
2
25
```

The difference is that on line 2 the numbers now have quotation marks around them. Even though they are numbers, because of the quotation marks JavaScript sees them as strings. And that means when it sorts them, it will sort them as if they are strings, so 1 is shown right before 11 the way that a will be shown before aa. In order to make the sorting take place properly, we have to use a custom function:

```
1 ▾ <script>
2 ▾ function my_custom_sort(a, b) {
3          // convert both to true numbers
4          a = a * 1;
5          b = b * 1;
6
7 ▾      if( a > b) {
8              return 1;
9          }
10 ▾     else if(a < b) {
11             return -1;
12         }
13 ▾     else {
14             return 0;
15         }
16     }
17     var numbers = ["1", "11", "2", "25"];
18     var sorted_numbers =
19         numbers.sort(my_custom_sort);
20     document.write(sorted_numbers.join('<br>'));
21 </script>
```

```
1
2
11
25
```

Above, **my_custom_sort** is a custom sorting function. All custom sorting functions take two values (**a** and **b**), compare them, then return a positive number, 0 or a negative number depending on how we want the sorting to be done. The value of these positive and negative numbers does not matter, all that JavaScript cares about is whether they are positive or negative. We use 1 and -1 in the example. What JavaScript does is get the first pair of values in the array (such as "1", "11", passes them to **my_custom_sort()**, then if the return value is -1, it means the first one should be first, if it is 0 it means they are equal and it does not matter which one is first, and if it is 1 it means the second one should be first. The first two lines of the function (4 and 5) convert the variables to "true" numbers by multiplying them by 1. This allows us to compare them as numbers rather than strings.

Below is an illustration of how JavaScript uses **my_custom_sort()** to do the sorting:

```
unsorted: ["1", "11", "2", "25"]
1st pass: my_custom_sort(1, 11).
    Return: -1.
    The array now: [1, 11, 2, 25]
2nd pass: my_custom_sort(11, 2).
    Return: 1.
    The array now: [1, 2, 11, 25]
3rd pass: my_custom_sort(11, 25).
    Return: -1.
    The array now: [1, 2, 11, 25]
Complete!
```

In reality we do not know how JavaScript does the sorting behind the scenes because there are various advanced algorithms used behind the scenes to speed up sorting. But when it comes to us programmers, all that we need to know is that custom sorting functions take two arguments and return either 1, 0 or -1.

On line 19 we have **numbers.sort(my_custom_sort)**. Even though **my_custom_sort** is a function, here we are using it without the usual parentheses because are only telling JavaScript the function's name, we do not want the function to be run on that line. JavaScript will run the function behind the scenes when it wants.

Custom sorting is an advanced part of programming and many programmers will have to use the Internet to look up the proper way to do it.

Instead of using a named function for sorting, we can use an anonymous function:

```
1  <script>
2  var numbers = ["1", "11", "2", "25"];
3  var sorted_numbers =
4      numbers.sort(function(a, b) {
5          // convert both to true numbers
6          a = a * 1;
7          b = b * 1;
8
9          if( a > b) {
10             return 1;
11         }
12         else if(a < b) {
13             return -1;
14         }
15         else {
16             return 0;
17         }
18     });
19  document.write(sorted_numbers.join('<br>'));
20  </script>
```

```
1
2
11
25
```

The sorting function can be shortened as follows. This is in fact how experienced programmers write sorting functions:

```
3    var sorted_numbers =
4 ▾      numbers.sort(function(a, b) {
5              // convert both to true numbers
6              a = a * 1;
7              b = b * 1;
8
9              return a - b;
10         });
```

Below is the same illustration as before updated to show how the shorter method works:

```
unsorted: ["1", "11", "2", "25"]
1st pass: function(1, 11).
    Return: 1 - 11 (-10).
    The array now: [1, 11, 2, 25]
2nd pass: function(11, 2).
    Return: 11 - 2 (9)
    The array now: [1, 2, 11, 25]
3rd pass: function(11, 25).
    Return: 11 - 25 (-14)
    The array now: [1, 2, 11, 25]
Complete!
```

Even though the numbers are now different, their positivity or negativity is exactly the same as before, and that is what matters.

In order to sort the numbers from largest to smallest, we can simply switch the places of the two variables in the sorting function:

```
i  1 ▾ <script>
   2   var numbers = ["1", "11", "2", "25"];                25
   3   var sorted_numbers =                                 11
   4 ▾     numbers.sort(function(a, b) {                    2
   5             // convert both to true numbers             1
   6             a = a * 1;
   7             b = b * 1;
   8
   9             return b - a;
   10        });
   11  document.write(sorted_numbers.join('<br>'));
   12  </script>
```

Below is an illustration of how this reverse sorting works:

```
unsorted: ["1", "11", "2", "25"]
1st pass: function(1, 11).
    Return: 11 - 1 (10).
    The array now: [11, 1, 2, 25]
2nd pass: function(1, 2).
    Return: 2 - 1 (1)
    The array now: [11, 2, 1, 25]
3rd pass: function(1, 25).
    Return: 25 - 1 (24)
    The array now: [11, 2, 25, 1]
4th pass: function(2, 25).
    Return: 25 - 2 (23).
    The array now: [11, 25, 2, 1]
5th pass: function (11, 25).
    Return: 25 - 11 (14).
    The array now: [25, 11, 2, 1]
Complete!
```

This time five passes were needed to complete the sort because the number 25 at the end has to be brought to the beginning one step at a time. Depending on the sorting algorithm used behind the scenes, a different number of passes could be needed.

Sorting arrays of objects

Below we have an array of objects representing a number of economists:

```
39 ▾ var economists = [
40 ▾     {
41           "name" : "Henry Charles Carey",
42           "death_year" : 1879,
43     },
44 ▾     {
45           "name" : "Erasmus Peshine Smith",
46           "death_year" : 1882,
47     },
48 ▾     {
49           "name" : "Adam Smith",
50           "death_year" : 1790,
51     },
52 ▾     {
53           "name" : "George Ernest Barnett",
54           "death_year" : 1938
55     }
56   ];
```

Below is our function to sort these economists by their names:

```
58   var sorted_by_name = economists.sort(
59 ▾     function(a, b) {
60 ▾         if(a.name < b.name) {
61               return -1;
62         }
63 ▾         else if(a.name > b.name) {
64               return 1;
65         }
66 ▾         else {
67               return 0;
68         }
69     }
70   )
71   print_array(sorted_by_name);
```

Here is the result:

```
[
{
"name" : Adam Smith
"death_year" : 1790
}
{
"name" : Erasmus Peshine Smith
"death_year" : 1882
}
{
"name" : George Ernest Barnett
"death_year" : 1938
}
{
"name" : Henry Charles Carey
"death_year" : 1879
}
]
```

Inside our sort function, we do not compare **a** and **b** directly. We compare **a.name** and **b.name**, because **a** and **b** represent individual objects inside the array and we interested in their **name** properties. Using the greater and small than signs with strings makes JavaScript compare the strings alphabetically, with "a" being "smaller" than "b", "b" being smaller than "c" and so on. Below is a simplified illustration of how the sorting is done:

```
unsorted: [{name: Henry}, {name: Erasmus}, {name: Adam}, {name: George}]
1st pass: function({name: Henry}, {name: Erasmus}).
    Henry is greater than Erasmus. Return 1.
    The array now: [{name: Erasmus}, {name: Henry}, {name: Adam}, {name: George}]
2nd pass: function({name: Henry}, {name: Adam}).
    Henry is greater than Adam. Return 1.
    The array now: [{name: Erasmus}, {name: Adam}, {name: Henry}, {name: George}]
3rd pass: function({name: Henry}, {name: George}).
    Henry is greater than George. Return 1.
    The array now: [{name: Erasmus}, {name: Adam}, {name: George}, {name: Henry}]
4th pass: function({name: Erasmus}, {name: Adam}).
    Erasmus is greater than Adam. Return 1.
    The array now: [{name: Adam}, {name: Erasmus}, {name: George}, {name: Henry}]
5th pass: function ({name: Erasmus}, {name: George}).
    Erasmus is smaller than Adam. Return -1.
    The array now: unchanged
6th pass: function ({name: George}, {name: Henry}).
    George is smaller than Henry. Return -1.
    The array now: unchanged
Complete!
```

Next we will sort the economists by their death dates:

```
44 ▾        {
45              "name" : "Erasmus Peshine Smith",
46              "death_year" : 1882,
47          },
48 ▾        {
49              "name" : "Adam Smith",
50              "death_year" : 1790,
51          },
52 ▾        {
53              "name" : "George Ernest Barnett",
54              "death_year" : 1938
55          }
56      ];
57
58      var sorted_by_death_year = economists.sort(
59 ▾        function(a, b) {
60              return a.death_year - b.death_year;
61          }
62      )
63      print_array(sorted_by_death_year);
64      </script>
65
66
67
```

```
[
{
"name" : Adam Smith
"death_year" : 1790
}
{
"name" : Henry Charles Carey
"death_year" : 1879
}
{
"name" : Erasmus Peshine Smith
"death_year" : 1882
}
{
"name" : George Ernest Barnett
"death_year" : 1938
}
]
```

Since we are comparing numbers, **a.death_year - b.death_year** on line 60 suffices for comparing them. If **a**'s death year is greater than **b**'s death, a positive number is returned, making **a** sorted after **b**. If **a**'s death year is smaller, a negative number is returned, making **a** get sorted before **b**. And if they are equal, 0 is returned, causing no change to their sorting. We can cause the economists to be sorted from the latest death to the earliest by changing line 60 as follows:

```
44 ▾        {
45              "name" : "Erasmus Peshine Smith",
46              "death_year" : 1882,
47          },
48 ▾        {
49              "name" : "Adam Smith",
50              "death_year" : 1790,
51          },
52 ▾        {
53              "name" : "George Ernest Barnett",
54              "death_year" : 1938
55          }
56      ];
57
58      var sorted_by_death_year = economists.sort(
59 ▾        function(a, b) {
60              return b.death_year - a.death_year;
61          }
62      )
63      print_array(sorted_by_death_year);
64      </script>
65
66
67
```

```
[
{
"name" : George Ernest Barnett
"death_year" : 1938
}
{
"name" : Erasmus Peshine Smith
"death_year" : 1882
}
{
"name" : Henry Charles Carey
"death_year" : 1879
}
{
"name" : Adam Smith
"death_year" : 1790
}
]
```

Filtering arrays

Filtering arrays allows us to filter out some of the elements of an array so that only those that we want will remain. We can do this using **for** loops, but the **filter()** function can be far more convenient and useful. Below we have an array of bird names and we only want the ones that start with a g:

```
 1  <script>
 2  var birds = ['duck', 'goose', 'swan', 'nene',
 3      'teal', 'pintail', 'scaup', 'eider',
 4      'scoter', 'maleo', 'chachalaca', 'guan',
 5      'curassow', 'partridge', 'grouse'];
 6
 7  var g_birds = birds.filter(function(bird) {
 8      if(bird[0] === 'g') {
 9          return true;
10      }
11      else {
12          return false;
13      }
14  });
15  document.write(g_birds.toString());
16  </script>
```

goose,guan,grouse

Similar to the **sort()** function, the **filter()** function can take an anonymous function that does the filtering for us. If this function returns true, it means the value should go through the filter. But if it returns false, it means the value should be filtered out.

Above, inside the anonymous function we check if the first character of bird is a g. If it is, we let it go through the filter. Otherwise we filter it out. The result is that **g_birds** ends up containing only those bird names that begin with g.

Below we have the economists from before. I have added a new property, **nationality**. We want to create a new array that has only the American economists:

```
39 ▾  var economists = [
40 ▾      {
41              "name" : "Henry Charles Carey",
42              "death_year" : 1879,
43              "nationality" : 'American',
44          },
45 ▾      {
46              "name" : "Erasmus Peshine Smith",
47              "death_year" : 1882,
48              "nationality" : 'American',
49          },
50 ▾      {
51              "name" : "Adam Smith",
52              "death_year" : 1790,
53              "nationality" : 'British',
54          },
55 ▾      {
56              "name" : "George Ernest Barnett",
57              "death_year" : 1938,
58              "nationality" : 'American',
59          }
60  ];
61  var american_economists = economists.filter(
62 ▾      function(single_economist) {
63              if(single_economist.nationality
64 ▾              === 'American') {
65                  return true;
66              }
67 ▾          else {
68                  return false;
69              }
70          }
71  );
72  print_array(american_economists);
73  </script>
```

```
[
{
"name" : Henry Charles Carey
"death_year" : 1879
"nationality" : American
}
{
"name" : Erasmus Peshine Smith
"death_year" : 1882
"nationality" : American
}
{
"name" : George Ernest Barnett
"death_year" : 1938
"nationality" : American
}
]
```

Next we will filter the economists to create an array of 19th century economists:

```
61  var 19_century_economists = economists.filter(
62 ▾      function(single_economist) {
63              if(single_economist.death_year >=
64              1800 && single_economist.death_year
65 ▾              <= 1900) {
66                  return true;
67              }
68 ▾          else {
69                  return false;
70              }
71          }
72  );
```

The above code actually causes an error:

```
⊗ ▸Uncaught SyntaxError: Invalid or unexpected token          VM10106:61
```

The error message is not very helpful. But since it gives us a line number on the far right (61), we know we have to look carefully at line 61. The problem on line 61 is that the variable **19_century_economists** has an invalid name because variable names cannot start with a number. Below is the corrected code:

```
55 ▾        {
56              "name" : "George Ernest Barnett",
57              "death_year" : 1938,
58              "nationality" : 'American',
59          }
60    ];
61    var nineteenth_century_economists =
62          economists.filter(
63 ▾            function(single_economist) {
64                  if(single_economist.death_year >=
65                      1800 && single_economist.death_year
66 ▾                  <= 1900) {
67                      return true;
68                  }
69 ▾              else {
70                      return false;
71                  }
72              }
73    );
74    print_array(nineteenth_century_economists);
75    </script>
```

```
[
{
"name" : Henry Charles Carey
"death_year" : 1879
"nationality" : American
}
{
"name" : Erasmus Peshine Smith
"death_year" : 1882
"nationality" : American
}
]
```

12. Events

When a user clicks on a word, button or image on a webpage, that click is seen by the browser and transmitted to JavaScript. In JavaScript, we can detect this "event" and do something in response to it.

There are many kinds of events, the most commonly used one being the **click** event. When you move your mouse over a webpage that is a **mousemove** event. When you scroll down a webpage, that is a **scroll** event. When your mouse enters the space above a certain HTML element (such as an image), that is a **mouseenter** event. In this chapter we will see the most important events in action.

In order to demonstrate events, we will start by creating a rectangle using HTML and CSS:

```
i  1 ▾ <div id="my-rectangle" style="height:
   2       50px; width:50px;
   3       border:5px solid #000;">
   4
   5    </div>
   6
   7
```

Above, I have used an HTML **<div>** element. I have given the element an **id** attribute of "my-rectangle". I could have called it "my-square" since it is a square. I chose to call it "my-rectangle" because later on we make changes to it that make it stop being a square.

In this way I have given this HTML element an "id" which allows me to refer to it later using JavaScript. Using the **style** attribute, I have also added some styling to the element (a border, a height and a width) to make it look like a rectangle. Similar to the **<script>** element that we have seen so much of, the **<div>** element has to be "closed" using a

</div> tag, because this is how the browser knows where this element's code ends and new code begins. On line 4 we can add contents inside the **<div>** element, as follows:

```
i  1 ▾ <div id="my-rectangle" style="height:
   2       50px; width:50px;
   3       border:5px solid #000;">
   4       Hello world!
   5   </div>
   6
```

```
Hello
world!
```

Now I will add a **<script>** tag below the **<div>** in order to add some JavaScript. The **<script>** tag has to be placed after the **<div>** because the code we write requires that the **<div>** should exist first. If your JavaScript code tries to deal with an HTML element that does not exist yet, you get an error.

```
i  1 ▾ <div id="my-rectangle" style="height:
   2       50px; width:50px;
   3       border:5px solid #000;">
   4       Hello world!
   5   </div>
   6
   7 ▾ <script>
   8       var my_rectangle = document.getElementById("my-rectangle");
   9   </script>
```

Above, on line 8 I use the built-in **document.getElementById()** function to get a hold of the **<div>** element I created earlier. As the name of the function suggests, it helps you "get" an "element" by its "id" in the "document". I place the element inside a variable named **my_rectangle**. The **my_rectangle** variable acts a bridge between JavaScript and HTML. When we do things to it, things happen to the HTML element in the document.

Next I will define a function that I will use later on:

```
   7 ▾ <script>
   8       var my_rectangle = document.getElementById("my-rectangle");
   9
  10 ▾    function write_out_a_response() {
  11           document.write('You just clicked the rectangle!');
  12       }
  13
  14   </script>
```

Above, the function on line 10-12 doesn't do anything yet. It is just a function definition that can be called later on.

Now, I will add the JavaScript code that watches out for clicks on the rectangle:

```
 7 ▾ <script>
 8       var my_rectangle = document.getElementById("my-rectangle");
 9
10 ▾     function write_out_a_response() {
11           document.write('You just clicked the rectangle!');
12       }
13
14       my_rectangle.addEventListener("click", write_out_a_response);
15
16   </script>
```

Our code is complete now. Above, I used the built-in **addEventListener()** function to tell JavaScript to run the **write_out_a_response** function when the user clicks on the rectangle. The **addEventListener()** function can only be used on a variable that contains a reference to an HTML element, as in the case of **my_rectangle**, which refers to the HTML element with the **id** of "my-rectangle".

The **addEventListener()** takes two arguments. The first one is the type of event we want to watch out for, in our case it is a **click** event. The second argument is the name of a function that we want to run when the event takes place. Note the way the function name does not have quotes around it. This is because we are giving **addEventListener()** the very function itself, not just its name. This will be made clearer later on.

Now, when I click the rectangle in the preview area, this is what happens:

You just clicked the rectangle!

The rectangle disappears and in its place we see the above message.

We now have an interactive program. A user clicks on something, the program respond's to the user's action.

The reason we no longer see the rectangle is that the **document.write()** statement on line 11 overwrites the entire document. The reason for this is technical but it is as follows for those interested: This did not happen in our past examples because those examples executed the **document.write()** statements as part of the document as it loaded. But if we delay the statement until a user action happens, for example until a user clicks on something as in the present example, then JavaScript ends up replacing the whole document with whatever the **document.write()** prints out. This is a problem with **document.write()** that makes it unfit for use with events.

At any rate, we need a better way of outputting stuff that does not overwrite the document. There are all kinds of ways of achieving this. For the present we will do it be inserting information write into the rectangle itself when a user clicks on it:

```
10 ▾    function write_out_a_response() {
11          var the_rectangle = document.getElementById("my-rectangle");
12          the_rectangle.innerHTML = 'You just clicked me!';
13      }
```

Above, I have updated the **write_out_a_response()** function to get a hold of the **my-rectangle <div>** element and to put some text inside it. On line 12 we use **the_rectangle.innerHTML**. This is how we refer to the inside contents of an HTML element when writing JavaScript code. The statement therefore means "replace the inner contents of the **my-rectangle** HTML element with the string **You just clicked me!**".

Here is the result in the preview area when I click the rectangle:

The text "overflows" outside the rectangle because the browser continues to respect the width and height we defined for the rectangle. If we try to put some stuff inside it that is too big, it will simply flow out of it. Below I have updated the HTML so that the rectangle now has a width of 100 pixels and no height definition:

```
i  1 ▾ <div id="my-rectangle" style="width:100px;
   2        border:5px solid #000;">
   3        Hello world!
   4  </div>
```

Hello world!

By not giving it a height, the browser automatically decides its height according to its contents. Now when I click on it, the rectangle expands to contain the full message:

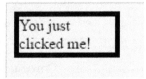

Below I have updated the **write_out_a_response()** function to do something a little more interesting:

```
 9 ▾    function write_out_a_response() {
10          var the_rectangle = document.getElementById("my-rectangle");
11          var old_contents = the_rectangle.innerHTML;
12          var new_contents = "You just clicked me!";
13          the_rectangle.innerHTML = old_contents + new_contents;
14      }
```

On 11 we get the contents of the rectangle and put it in a variable. On 12 we create a new variable, and on line 13 we put the two together and put them back inside the rectangle. This means that every time we click the rectangle, the sentence "You just clicked me!" is added to whatever is already inside it. Below is the result in the preview area after I clicked the rectangle four times:

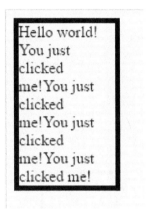

Next, we will change **write_out_a_response()** to clone the rectangle every time a user clicks on it:

```
10 ▾    function write_out_a_response() {
11          var the_rectangle = document.getElementById("my-rectangle");
12          var new_rectangle = the_rectangle.cloneNode();
13          document.body.appendChild(new_rectangle);
14      }
```

On line 12 above we use **the_rectangle.cloneNode()** to create a "clone" of the rectangle element and we put it inside **new_rectangle**. This only creates a clone in JavaScript, nothing happens to the HTML document yet. We next have to tell JavaScript where to put the clone that we just created. We do that on line 13 using **document.body.appendChild()**. This function takes an HTML element and places it at the end of the document. Line 13 therefore inserts the cloned rectangle into the document at its very end. Here is the result when I click the rectangle twice:

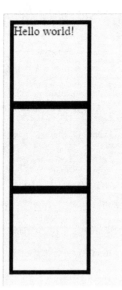

The reason the cloned rectangles are empty and do not contain the "Hello world!" sentence is because the **cloneNode()** function only copies the element itself, not its *contents*. In order to also copy the contents, we have to pass a boolean **true** to it as follows:

```
12    var new_rectangle = the_rectangle.cloneNode(true);
```

Here is the result:

A real-world program

In this section we will discuss how to build a small interactive program using what we have learned so far. Here is the code that we will start with:[6]

```
 1  <html>
 2      <head>
 3          <script>
 4          function submit() {
 5              document.getElementById("output").innerHTML =
 6              'You just clicked submit!';
 7          }
 8
 9          </script>
10      </head>
11      <body>
12          <textarea id="input"></textarea>
13          <br>
14          <button onclick="submit()">Submit</button>
15          <br>
16          <div id="output"></div>
17      </body>
18  </html>
```

Here is the result when we run the code:

You can put the above code in a file ending with the html extension in order to use it in a browser, as follows (I have named it program.html):

1	10/6/2018 1:31 PM	File folder	
program.html	10/6/2018 1:30 PM	Chrome HTML Do…	1 KB
text_analyzer.txt	10/1/2018 5:32 PM	Text Document	3 KB

When opening this file in Chrome, here is the result:

---

[6] You can copy this code from my website at http://hawramani.com/?p=66687

If you put the code in a file and open it in a browser as shown above, you will have to click the reload button every time you make a change to the code.

The code we have is mostly HTML code that creates a text area and a button. This is not the place to explain how HTML works, but if you look at the code for the button on line 14, you will notice that it has an **onclick** property that refers to a JavaScript function:

```
14            <button onclick="submit()">Submit</button>
```

We already covered how to add an event listener to an HTML element using the **addEventListener()** function. The above accomplishes the exact same thing; it is just another way of adding an event listener to an HTML element, but rather than having to do it in a JavaScript section of code, we add the event as an attribute of the HTML element itself. Note that the attribute is "onclick" rather than "click".

The **submit()** function is defined above it on lines 4-7:

```
4 ▾    function submit() {
5          document.getElementById("output").innerHTML =
6          'You just clicked submit!';
7      }
```

This **submit()** function will be run every time a user clicks on the button. What the code of the function does on lines 5-6 is find an HTML element with the id of "output" (see line 16) then it replaces its contents with the text "You just clicked submit!".

Below is what shows up in the preview area when I click the submit button:

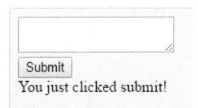

Below I have updated the **submit()** function to print out the current date and time when someone clicks the Submit button:

```
4 ▾    function submit() {
5          var date_string = new Date().toLocaleString();
6
7          document.getElementById("output").innerHTML =
8          'Current date and time: '
9              + date_string;
10     }
```

On line 5, we create a JavaScript **Date** object using the special **new** "operator". **Date** is a built-in JavaScript construct that allows us to access functionalities related to date and time. The statement **new Date()** means "create a **Date** object and return it." But instead of putting this returned object in a variable, we immediately access a function that the object has, which is the **toLocaleString()** function, which returns a string that represents the current date and time.

To clarify further, below is line 5 broken into two lines:

```
var date_object = new Date();
var date_string = date_object.toLocaleString();
```

Here is the result when we click Submit:

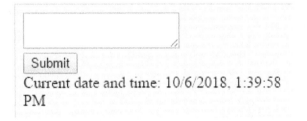

Moving on, we update the **submit()** function so that it greets the user if they put their name in the empty box you see in the preview area:

```
4 ▾    function submit() {
5          var input = document.getElementById("input").value;
6          document.getElementById("output").innerHTML =
7          'Hello ' + input + '!';
8      }
```

Below I put my first name in the box then clicked Submit:

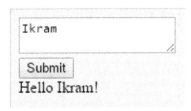

The statement **document.getElementById("input").value** retrieves whatever text is in the empty box. We have already seen **document.getElementById()** before. In this case we are retrieving the HTML element that has an id of "input", then we are accessing the **value** property of this retrieved element. Note that only a few HTML elements have a **value** property.

Below I wrote "Fred Flintstone" in the input box and press Submit:

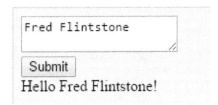

Below I update **submit()** so that it is now a function that converts a person's height to centimeters. The user is supposed to enter a height in feet and inches and will be shown their height in centimeters once they click Submit:

```
 4 ▾    function submit() {
 5          var input = document.getElementById("input").value;
 6          var measures = input.split(" ");
 7          var feet = measures[0];
 8          var feet_numbers = feet[0];
 9          var inches = measures[1];
10          var inches_numbers = inches.replace('"', '');
11          var inches_numbers = inches_numbers * 1;
12          var total_inches = (feet_numbers * 12) + inches_numbers;
13          var centimeters = total_inches * 2.54;
14          var centimeters_rounded = Math.floor(centimeters);
15
16          document.getElementById("output").innerHTML =
17          'Your height in centimeters: ' + centimeters_rounded ;
18      }
```

Here is the result when I enter a height and click Submit:

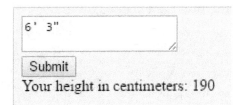

Below is the same function with explanatory comments added:

```
 4 ▾      function submit() {
 5            var input = document.getElementById("input").value;
 6            // split 6' 3" into an array
 7            var measures = input.split(" ");
 8            // feet contains the string 6'
 9            var feet = measures[0];
10            // feet_numbers contains 6 (we get first character)
11            var feet_numbers = feet[0];
12            // 3"
13            var inches = measures[1];
14            // 3 (we replace quotation mark with nothing to delete it)
15            var inches_numbers = inches.replace('"', '');
16            // multiply by number to force JavaScript to
17            // treat it as a number
18            var inches_numbers = inches_numbers * 1;
19            var total_inches = (feet_numbers * 12) + inches_numbers;
20            var centimeters = total_inches * 2.54;
21            var centimeters_rounded = Math.floor(centimeters);
22
23            document.getElementById("output").innerHTML =
24            'Your height in centimeters: ' + centimeters_rounded ;
25      }
```

On line 15 we use the **replace()** function without using a regular expression, as this function can also take strings as its first argument. The statement **replace('"', '')** makes JavaScript find all double quotation marks and replace them with nothing, meaning that they all get deleted. When we pass a string to **replace()** rather than a regular expression, the replacement will be done globally, so there is no need for the **g** modifier. In fact we cannot use modifiers in **replace()** unless we are using regular expressions.

Mouseover and mouseout events

In JavaScript we can attach multiple events to the same element. In this section we will use the **mouseover** and **mouseout** events on the rectangle from earlier. The **mouseover** event takes place when a user's mouse enters the space occupied an HTML element, while the **mouseout** event is its opposite; it takes place (or "fires") when the user's mouse leaves the space occupied by an element. Below is the code we will use:

```
 7 ▾  <script>
 8 ▾      function say_in() {
 9             the_rectangle = document.getElementById("my-rectangle");
10             the_rectangle.innerHTML = 'Mouse is inside';
11         }
12 ▾      function say_out() {
13             the_rectangle = document.getElementById("my-rectangle");
14             the_rectangle.innerHTML = "Mouse is outside.";
15         }
16
17         var my_rectangle = document.getElementById("my-rectangle");
18         my_rectangle.addEventListener("mouseover", say_in);
19         my_rectangle.addEventListener("mouseout", say_out);
20
21     </script>
```

Above, we attach two separate events to the rectangle on lines 18 and 19. Each event calls one of the functions defined above. Here is what the rectangle looks like originally, when the page first loads:

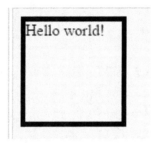

When I hover my mouse above the rectangle, the rectangle's text changes as follows:

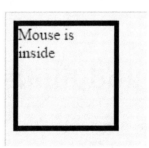

And as soon as my mouse leaves the rectangle, the text changes as follows:

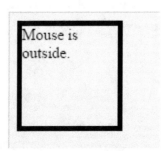

JavaScript menus

Many websites use menus that integrate JavaScript functionality. Below is a screenshot of the Open Library website. When I click "Browse", the vertical menu that you see opens up.

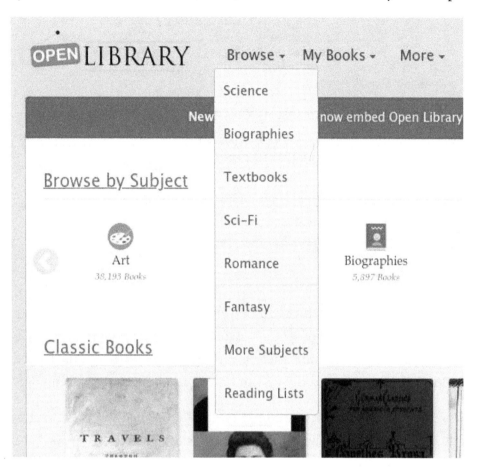

We will now recreate a very simple replica of the above menu. Below we have two HTML elements, a "browse-button" element that will function as our button, and a "sub-menu" element that will function as the menu that opens up when a user clicks "Browse". In a real menu the menu items (like "Science") would be links to other webpages. But to keep things simple we will merely write "Science" and so on without worrying about links.

```
1    <div id="browse-button">Browse</div>
2 ▾  <div id="sub-menu">
3        Science<br>
4        Biographies<br>
5        Textbooks<br>
6    </div>
7
```

Browse
Science
Biographies
Textbooks

As you can see in the preview area, currently everything shows up. We want only "Browse" to show up, so that a user can click it to view the rest of the words. In order to achieve that, we will add a **style** attribute to the "sub-menu" element (line 3 below):

```
i  1   <div id="browse-button">Browse</div>
   2 ▾ <div id="sub-menu"                          Browse
   3       style="display:none;">
   4       Science<br>
   5       Biographies<br>
   6       Textbooks<br>
   7   </div>
```

As you can see in the preview area, now only the word "Browse" shows up. The "sub-menu" element exists; it is just hidden at the moment. We will JavaScript to make up show up when we want. Below I have added the JavaScript to accomplish that:

```
 9 ▾ <script>
10       var browse_button = document.getElementById('browse-button');
11 ▾    browse_button.addEventListener('click', function() {
12           var sub_menu = document.getElementById('sub-menu');
13           sub_menu.style.display = 'block';
14       });
15   </script>
```

On lines 11-14, we use the **addEventListener()** to attach a click event to the "Browse" button. Instead of passing it a function's name as its second argument, we pass it an anonymous function. This does not make a difference to its functionality; it is just more convenient since it helps you avoid the task of having to name your function.

Inside the anonymous function we get a hold of the "sub-menu" element and on line 13 we change its **style.display** attribute to **block**. This causes it to show up.

Here is the result when click "Browse":

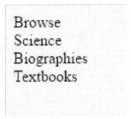

We are only half-way done. In order for it to be a proper menu, the sub menu should go away when a user clicks "Browse" again. In order to accomplish that we make the following changes to the anonymous function:

```
11 ▾        browse_button.addEventListener('click', function() {
12               var sub_menu = document.getElementById('sub-menu');
13 ▾             if(sub_menu.style.display === 'none') {
14                   sub_menu.style.display = 'block';
15               }
16 ▾             else if(sub_menu.style.display === 'block') {
17                   sub_menu.style.display = 'none';
18               }
19          });
```

Above, inside the anonymous function we now have conditional blocks. On line 13 we check if the sub menu is not showing up, in which case we cause it to show up on line 14. But if it is already showing up, we cause it to stop showing up on line 17. In this way we "toggle" the menu.

Below I have changed the menu so that now the sub menu shows up when a user's mouse is over the word "Browse". When they take their mouse away, the sub menu goes away. To accomplish that I have used two event listeners:

```
 9 ▾  <script>
10         var browse_button = document.getElementById('browse-button');
11 ▾       browse_button.addEventListener('mouseover', function() {
12             var sub_menu = document.getElementById('sub-menu');
13             sub_menu.style.display = 'block';
14         });
15 ▾       browse_button.addEventListener('mouseout', function() {
16             var sub_menu = document.getElementById('sub-menu');
17             sub_menu.style.display = 'none';
18         });
19     </script>
```

Note that the above code is not sufficient to make a functioning menu because as soon as a user moves their mouse pointer to the sub menu (for example if they were intending to click "Science") the sub menu goes away, so that they never get the opportunity to actually click anything in the sub menu. In order to make it function properly we will need to use some complex logic which is beyond the scope of this book.

Using "this" with events

We saw the **this** keyword in the coffee robot example. This keyword is extremely useful when dealing with events. Below we have some CSS and HTML that creates four rectangles as can be seen in the preview area. The **<style>** tag at the top allows us to add "styling" to HTML elements. In this case we are adding borders, margins and other styling using the CSS language which is beyond the scope of this book.

```
i  1 ▾ <style>
   2 ▾     div {
   3            border:5px solid #000;
   4            float:left;
   5            margin: 10px;
   6            padding:10px;
   7        }
   8  </style>
   9
  10 ▾ <div>
  11        Rectangle 1
  12  </div>
  13 ▾ <div>
  14        Rectangle 2
  15  </div>
  16 ▾ <div>
  17        Rectangle 3
  18  </div>
  19 ▾ <div>
  20        Rectangle 4
  21  </div>
```

Next we will add a JavaScript statement to get a hold of all the rectangles in one variable:

```
23 ▾ <script>
24        var all_rectangles = document.querySelectorAll('div');
25
26  </script>
```

Above, we are using **document.querySelectorAll()**. This function retrieves all HTML elements that share a certain characteristic. In this case, we are retrieving all HTML elements that are **<div>** tags.

Next we will define the function that we want to run when a user clicks on any of the rectangles:

```
25 ▾    function change_background() {
26          this.style.background = 'red';
27       }
```

The **change_background()** function simply changes the background color of the clicked element to red. On line 26 we use **this** to refer to the currently clicked element without caring what element it is. You will see why this is useful below.

We next add event listeners to the rectangles using a **for** loop:

```
29 ▾    for(var i = 0; i < all_rectangles.length; i++) {
30          all_rectangles[i].addEventListener("click", change_background);
31       }
```

The loop goes over the **all_rectangles** variable and adds an event listener to each rectangle using the **addEventListener()** function. We pass **change_background** to the **addEventListener()** function as its second argument on line 30, meaning that the **change_background()** function will run whenever a user clicks on any of the rectangles.

Below is the result in the preview area when I click on the first rectangle:

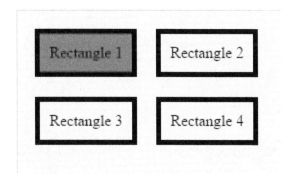

Below I have clicked on the fourth rectangle:

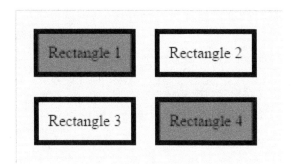

Thanks to using **this** inside the **change_background()** function, JavaScript intelligently applies the background change to the rectangle we have clicked and not to the other ones.

Below I have updated the JavaScript so that now the background of a rectangle changes when a user hovers their mouse pointer over it. However, I have also added the twist that when a user's mouse pointer leaves a rectangle, the background of the rectangle is reset to transparent:

```
23 ▾  <script>
24        var all_rectangles = document.querySelectorAll('div');
25 ▾      function change_background() {
26            this.style.background = 'red';
27        }
28 ▾      function reset_background() {
29            this.style.background = 'transparent';
30        }
31
32 ▾      for(var i = 0; i < all_rectangles.length; i++) {
33            all_rectangles[i].addEventListener("mouseover", change_background);
34            all_rectangles[i].addEventListener("mouseout", reset_background);
35        }
36
37    </script>
```

On line 33 we pass **change_background** to **addEventListerner()**, while on line 34 we pass the new function **reset_background**. Try to take the time to read the above code carefully until you fully understanding how it works.

13. Cookies

You may have seen those annoying notifications on certain websites that tell you that the site uses cookies. Those notifications are required by European Union privacy laws. Cookies allow websites to store information about the current user on the user's own machine. For example, a news website may allow you to change the size of the text in their articles and store your preference in a cookie. When you come back to their site the next day, the site uses its cookie to remember your preferred text size. In this way you do not have to go through the hassle of changing the text size every time you visit the site. The site "remembers" your preferred size. There is nothing sinister about this type of cookie. There is however another type of cookie known as a "third-party cookie" that is used by sites like Facebook and Google to track your online activities *even when you are not on their website*. We will not go into further details about that since it is beyond the scope of this book.

 Below, we have the first sentence of George Eliot's *Middlemarch* in a **<p>** tag (which stands for "paragraph"):

```
1 ▾  <p>Who that cares much to know the history of man, and how the
2       mysterious mixture behaves under the varying experiments of Time,
3       has not dwelt, at least briefly, on the life of Saint Theresa,
4       has not smiled with some gentleness at the thought of the little
5       girl walking forth one morning hand-in-hand with her still
6       smaller brother, to go and seek martyrdom in the country of
7       the Moors?
8    </p>
```

We will now add buttons to enable the user to increase or decrease the size of the text. We will not use anything fancy, just unstyled **<div>** tags as follows:

```
 9    <div>+ Increase size</div>
10    <div>- Decrease size</div>
```

Here is what the preview area looks line now:

Who that cares much to know the history of man, and how the mysterious mixture behaves under the varying experiments of Time, has not dwelt, at least briefly, on the life of Saint Theresa, has not smiled with some gentleness at the thought of the little girl walking forth one morning hand-in-hand with her still smaller brother, to go and seek martyrdom in the country of the Moors?

+ Increase size
- Decrease size

We will start our JavaScript with a variable that keeps track of the current size setting in pixels. It is currently set to 16, because that is the font size that the preview area uses by default.

```
12 ▾  <script>
13      var current_size_setting = 16;
```

We will next add the function that changes font sizes when a user clicks on either of the two buttons.

```
15 ▾  function change_size() {
16        var the_paragraph = document.querySelectorAll('p')[0];
17    }
```

Above, we have a barebones function for now that only retrieves the paragraph without doing anything to it yet. It uses the **querySelectorAll()** function to retrieve all **<p>** tags in the document. But since we are dealing with only one **<p>** tag, at the end of the statement we have put a **[0]** to access the first and only element returned by the function (since the function always returns an array-like result even if there is only one element). To clarify, here is the same statement broken into two lines:

```
15 ▾  function change_size() {
16        var all_paragraphs = document.querySelectorAll('p');
17        var the_paragraph = all_paragraphs[0];
18    }
```

Next, we will put **this** into a new variable just for clarity;

```
15 ▾  function change_size() {
16         var all_paragraphs = document.querySelectorAll('p');
17         var the_paragraph = all_paragraphs[0];
18
19         var current_button = this;
20     }
```

The **current_button** variable refers to the button the user has clicked, which is going to be either the "Increase size" button or the "Decrease size" button. Putting this inside a variable does not change how it works, but it makes the code easier to read since **this** is vague and can be hard to interpret, especially if you are dealing with a long piece of code.

Next we will add an **if** statement to the function:

```
19         var current_button = this;
20 ▾      if(current_button.innerHTML === '+ Increase size') {
21
22         }
23 ▾      else {
24
25         }
```

In the if statement's condition we check the **innerHTML** attribute of the button to find out whether the current button is the button for increasing or decreasing text size (since we are going to be using the **change_size()** function for both increasing and decreasing text size). Any code we place on line 21 will run when the user clicked on "Increase size", while any code we put on line 24 will run if the user clicked on "Decrease size".

Below we have added the finishing touches to **change_size()**:

```
12 ▾  <script>
13     var current_size_setting = 16;
14
15 ▾  function change_size() {
16         var all_paragraphs = document.querySelectorAll('p');
17         var the_paragraph = all_paragraphs[0];
18
19         var current_button = this;
20 ▾      if(current_button.innerHTML === '+ Increase size') {
21             current_size_setting = current_size_setting + 2;
22             the_paragraph.style.fontSize = current_size_setting + 'px';
23         }
24 ▾      else {
25             current_size_setting = current_size_setting - 2;
26             the_paragraph.style.fontSize = current_size_setting + 'px';
27         }
28     }
```

On line 21 we are using the **current_size_setting** variable that was defined *outside* the function (note how there is no **var** in front of it). This is important because by having this variable outside the **change_size()** function, the variable continues to exist even after the function ends. Next time the **change_size()** function runs, it will still access the very same **current_size_setting** variable from before. The **current_size_setting** variable continues to "live" behind the scenes as long as the document is open in a browser.

On line 21 we increase the **current_size_setting** variable's value by 2. We could have increased it by 1 instead, but 2 causes is a more visible change in the font size. On line 22 we update the font size of the paragraph using **the_paragraph.style.fontSize**. Note that this will not work if we merely pass it a number. It has to end with a unit, such as "px" (which stands for pixels, which is a unit of measurement for text sizes and other things). This is why we have **+ 'px'** at the end of the statement.

On lines 25-26 we have the counterpart for the above code, this time for decreasing the font size.

Next we have the code for attaching the event listeners to the buttons:

```
30    var change_size_buttons = document.querySelectorAll("div");
31
32 ▾  for(var i = 0; i < change_size_buttons.length; i++) {
33        change_size_buttons[i].addEventListener("click", change_size);
34    }
35    </script>
```

Here is the result in the preview area after I clicked "Increase size" once:

Who that cares much to know the history of man, and how the mysterious mixture behaves under the varying experiments of Time, has not dwelt, at least briefly, on the life of Saint Theresa, has not smiled with some gentleness at the thought of the little girl walking forth one morning hand-in-hand with her still smaller brother, to go and seek martyrdom in the country of the Moors?

+ Increase size
- Decrease size

If I click it again, the size increases more:

Who that cares much to know the history of man, and how the mysterious mixture behaves under the varying experiments of Time, has not dwelt, at least briefly, on the life of Saint Theresa, has not smiled with some gentleness at the thought of the little girl walking forth one morning hand-in-hand with her still smaller brother, to go and seek martyrdom in the country of the Moors?

+ Increase size
- Decrease size

We now have a fully functional system for allowing users to increase and decrease the text size of this paragraph.

Next we will use cookies to store the user's text size preference so that even if they close the page and open it again, the document continues to remember the text size they set the paragraph at.

Note that not all browsers all you to set cookies when dealing with local files. If you are using JS Tinker, cookies will only work if you have accessed JS Tinker through a website. If download JS Tinker and open it locally, cookies will not work except in certain browsers (such as version 53 of Firefox).

First, here is a function I have added to the top of the script to check whether cookies are enabled or not:[7]

```
12 ▾ <script>
13 ▾     function areCookiesEnabled() {
14          document.cookie = "verify=1";
15          if(document.cookie.length >= 1
16 ▾          && document.cookie.indexOf("verify=1") !== -1) {
17              return true;
18          }
19          return false;
20      }
21 ▾     if(areCookiesEnabled()) {
22          document.write('We have cookies!');
23      }
```

---

[7] You can copy the code from my website at http://hawramani.com/?p=66687.

Above, we use the function **areCookiesEnabled()** to check whether we can create cookies or not. This function tries to create a cookie on line 14 and on lines 15-16 checks whether the cookie was created or not.

The statement **document.cookie = "verify=1"** on line 14 creates a cookie with the name of **verify** and with the value of **1**. On line 15, the condition **document.cookie.length >= 1** checks whether any cookies exist at all. On line 16, we specifically check whether a cookie exists with the name of **verify** and the value of **1**.

Here is the result in the preview area when I run the above code:

Who that cares much to know the history of man, and how the mysterious mixture behaves under the varying experiments of Time, has not dwelt, at least briefly, on the life of Saint Theresa, has not smiled with some gentleness at the thought of the little girl walking forth one morning hand-in-hand with her still smaller brother, to go and seek martyrdom in the country of the Moors?

+ Increase size
- Decrease size
We have cookies!

Note the sentence "We have cookies!" at the bottom.

The **document.cookie** variable is actually just a simple string variable that holds all cookies. We can even print it out, as follows:

```
25      document.write('<br>');
26      document.write(document.cookie);
```

Here is the result:

+ Increase size
- Decrease size
We have cookies!
verify=1

As you can see above, **document.cookie** merely contains the string **verify=1**. Which was created by **areCookiesEnabled()** earlier.

We will next add a function for creating cookies. We already saw that we can create cookies merely by writing **document.cookie = "cookie_name=cookie_value "**. The problem with cookies created this way is that they are deleted once the user leaves the document, which rather defeats the purpose of cookies. In order to create proper cookies, we will use a **setCookie()** function as follows:

```
26 ▾    function setCookie(name,value,days) {
27          var expires = "";
28 ▾        if (days) {
29              var date = new Date();
30              date.setTime(date.getTime() + (days*24*60*60*1000));
31              expires = "; expires=" + date.toUTCString();
32              console.log(expires);
33          }
34 ▾        if(!value) {
35              value = "";
36          }
37          cookie = name + "=" + value  + expires + "; path=/";
38          document.cookie = cookie;
39      }
```

Dealing with cookies is such a tiresome business that programmers simply copy a few good cookie-related functions from the Internet without bothering about how they work. I will try to explain how the function works, but you shouldn't worry too much about it since you can use it whether you understand it or not. Some of the discussion will get quite technical, so feel free to merely skim the explanations on how cookie functions work. The **setCookie()** function takes three arguments: the name of the cookie, its value, and the number of days the cookie should be stored on the user's computer. On lines 28-32 the function creates a string that represents the cookie's expiry date. The expiry date is calculated based on the number of days that are passed to the function. On lines 33-35 we set the **value** variable to an empty string if it is a "falsy" value like **null**, **NaN**, zero or **false**. This helps avoid unexpected behavior that comes about if you try to store such values in cookies. Note that this means you cannot store the number zero in a cookie. If you are storing numbers in a cookie, if you have to store zero then simply store an empty string and later check if the cookie's value is an empty string. If so, you can then assume it is a zero.

On line 36 we store the actual cookie. Here is what the **cookie** would look like if we were to print it out after calling the function as **setCookie("cookie_name", "cookie_value", 365)**:

```
cookie_name=cookie_value; expires=Fri, 22 Nov 2019 17:36:22 GMT; path = /
```

If we print out **document.cookies** now to see the cookies we have, here is what we get:

+ Increase size
- Decrease size
We have cookies!
verify=1; cookie_name=cookie_value

Even though we created an expiry date and a "path" for the cookie in **setCookie()**, when printing out the cookies we only see the cookie's name and value because, for whatever reason, JavaScript is designed to prevent us from accessing cookies' expiry dates and paths.

The path determines which pages of a website the cookie will apply to. If the path is a forward slash as it is above, that means the cookie will apply to the entire website, meaning that every page of the website will be able to access the cookie and update it.

Next we will discuss the **getCookie()** function that we will use for getting the values of cookies we have already stored:

```
40    function getCookie(name) {
41        var result = document.cookie.match("\\b" + name + "=([^;]*)\\b");
42        if(result) {
43            return result[1];
44        }
45        else {
46            return null;
47        }
48    };
```

The above uses a sophisticated regular expression on line 41 to find out whether the **document.cookie** variable contains a cookie with that matches the **name** argument passed to the function. Explaining how the regular expression works is beyond our scope.

On line 42 we check if we have a **result**, and if so, we return the first match using **result[1]**. And if there is no result, meaning we did not find a cookie with that name, then we return **null** on line 46.

We will now update the **change_size()** function to store the user's size preference in a cookie:

```
52 ▾    function change_size() {
53          var all_paragraphs = document.querySelectorAll('p');
54          var the_paragraph = all_paragraphs[0];
55
56          var current_button = this;
57 ▾        if(current_button.innerHTML === '+ Increase size') {
58              current_size_setting = current_size_setting + 2;
59              the_paragraph.style.fontSize = current_size_setting + 'px';
60          }
61 ▾        else {
62              current_size_setting = current_size_setting - 2;
63              the_paragraph.style.fontSize = current_size_setting + 'px';
64          }
65          setCookie('size-preference', current_size_setting, 365);
66      }
```

On line 65 we are storing a cookie named size-preference and in it we store the value of **current_size_setting**. This means that every time the user changes the size of the text, we update the cookie to reflect the new size.

We now need a way to restore the user's size preference when they first open the page. Remember that above the **change_size()** function we defined the original value for **current_size_setting**, as follows:

```
50      var current_size_setting = 16;
51
52 ▾    function change_size() {
```

We will now add a cookie-related section underneath line 50:

```
50      var current_size_setting = 16;
51      var cookie_value = getCookie('size-preference');
52 ▾    if(cookie_value !== null && cookie_value !== "") {
53          current_size_setting = cookie_value;
54          current_size_setting = current_size_setting * 1;
55          var all_paragraphs = document.querySelectorAll('p');
56          var the_paragraph = all_paragraphs[0];
57          the_paragraph.style.fontSize = current_size_setting + 'px';
58      }
59
60 ▾    function change_size() {
```

On line 51 we try to retrieve the cookie's value. On line 52 we check if the cookie is not null and not an empty string, and if so we use its value. On line 54 we multiply **current_size_setting** by 1 in order to force it to become a number (since all values from cookies are strings by default). On lines 55-58 we update the paragraph's **style.fontSize** property in order to contain the size preference we got from the cookie.

Note that the above cookie-related code only runs once; when the page loads.

Now each time I increase or decrease the text size, if I type **document.cookie** in the JavaScript console I can see the new size reflected there:

```
>>  document.cookie;
<-  "verify=1; size-preference=26"
>>  document.cookie;
<-  "verify=1; size-preference=24"
>>  document.cookie;
<-  "verify=1; size-preference=22"
>> document.cookie;
```

Deleting cookies

Deleting a cookie is as simple as changing its expiry date so that the browser thinks the cookie has expired:

```
49 ▾    function deleteCookie(name) {
50           var past_date = new Date(1976, 8, 16);
51           var expired_string = 'expires=' + past_date.toUTCString();
52           var expired_cookie = name + '=; ' + expired_string + '; path=/';
53           document.cookie = expired_cookie;
54       }
```

Above on line 50 we use **new Date()** to create a JavaScript **Date** object set to represent a day in 1976. On line 51 we create a string variable that contains the full cookie-format definition for the expired date. On line 52 we create the full expired cookie. Note the "path" at the end, this has to exactly match the path the cookie was created with. The cookie value does not matter, note that it is empty above.

On line 53 we perform the deletion by storing the expired cookie, which causes the original cookie to be replaced by the expired cookie, which is then immediately deleted by the browser. Note that **document.cookie** is a special variable, as we have already seen when we write **document.cookie =** this only affects one cookie at a time.

Where to go next

At this point you have mastered the basic concepts of programming in JavaScript. You can go on to learn any language you choose, be it C, PHP (used by web servers), Python or Swift (used by Apple apps) and you will find most of the concepts already familiar.

If your goal is to go on to build websites, you have to master what is known as a technology stack. You will need HTML and CSS for building web pages (along with JavaScript). The author's *HTML & CSS for Complete Beginners* is a user-friendly guide to these two languages.

You will also need a server scripting language, such as PHP, Ruby or Python. You will also need some knowledge of the database language SQL.

WordPress is a great system for beginners who want to build websites. It already has everything set up (HTML, CSS, JavaScript, PHP and MySQL) and it can allow you to get a website up and running in minutes. I highly recommend using WordPress or another framework as a learning tool because tinkering with already-built systems is a great way of mastering programming. The author's *Cloud Computing for Complete Beginners* teaches how to get your very own Linux web server and get a WordPress-based website working on it. If you want to do some "real" web development work then this is a great place to start, since once you are done you will have a fully functional website on the Internet.

If you want to build games to be played on Android and iOS devices, you can check out the Unity framework. This is a program that allows you to build a game using visual tools and the C# (C-Sharp) language. When the game is ready, it can be "exported" to both Android and iOS without having to worry too much about the differences between these two systems.

If your goal is to build apps (not games) for mobile devices, React Native is the most popular tool right now and uses JavaScript as its basis and is used by some of the biggest tech companies.

If you are some sort of business manager and wish to put your new programming skills to good use, you can import spreadsheets into Google Spreadsheets then use JavaScript to run little programs on the spreadsheet to do all sorts of advanced calculations (do a web search for "google spreadsheet scripting").

If you are interested in a more academic study of programming, you can search for books on object oriented programming, data structures and algorithms.

www.ingramcontent.com/pod-product-compliance
Lightning Source LLC
LaVergne TN
LVHW081657050326
832903LV00026B/1798